WAITING IN THE WINGS

A Play in Three Acts

by

NOËL COWARD

SAMUEL FRENCH

LONDON

NEW YORK TORONTO SYDNEY HOLLYWOOD

WAITING IN THE WINGS

Produced by F.E.S. (PLAYS) LTD in association with Michael Redgrave Productions Ltd, at the Duke of York's Theatre, London, on the 7th September 1960, with the following cast of characters—

(in the order of their appearance)

BONITA BELGRAVE	⎫	*Maidie Andrews*
CORA CLARKE		*Una Venning*
MAUD MELROSE		*Norah Blaney*
MAY DAVENPORT	⎬ residents at "The Wings"	*Marie Löhr*
ALMINA CLARE		*Mary Clare*
ESTELLE CRAVEN		*Edith Day*
DEIRDRE O'MALLEY	⎭	*Maureen Delany*
PERRY LASCOE, the Secretary		*Graham Payn*
SYLVIA ARCHIBALD, the Superintendent		*Margot Boyd*
MR OSGOOD MEEKER		*Lewis Casson*
LOTTA BAINBRIDGE		*Sybil Thorndike*
DORA, her dresser		*Betty Hare*
DOREEN, the maid		*Jean Conroy*
SARITA MYRTLE, a Resident		*Nora Nicholson*
ZELDA FENWICK, a Journalist		*Jessica Dunning*
DR JEVONS		*Eric Hillyard*
ALAN BENNET, Lotta's son		*William Hutt*
TOPSY BASKERVILLE		*Molly Lumley*

Directed by MARGARET WEBSTER
Scenery and costumes by MOTLEY

SYNOPSIS OF SCENES

The action of the Play passes in the lounge of "The Wings", a charity home for retired actresses, in the Thames Valley, not far from Bourne End

ACT I

SCENE 1   A Sunday afternoon in June
SCENE 2   3 a.m. on a Monday morning, a month later

ACT II

SCENE 1   A Sunday afternoon in the following September
SCENE 2   Several hours later
SCENE 3   A week later

ACT III

SCENE 1   The evening of Christmas Day
SCENE 2   A Sunday afternoon in the following June

Time—the present

Photograph by Angus McBean

WAITING IN THE WINGS

ACT I

SCENE I

SCENE—*The lounge of "The Wings", a small charity home for retired actresses, in the Thames Valley, not far from Bourne End. A Sunday afternoon in June.*

"The Wings" differs from organizations of its kind in that it provides only for those who have been stars or leading ladies and who, through age, lack of providence, misfortune, etc., have been reduced to poverty. Some of these have been granted a pension of four pounds a week by the King George's Pension Fund; others have small, pitifully small, incomes of their own. No actress under the age of sixty is eligible for admittance to the Home. "The Wings" is subscribed to by public funds and was founded in 1925 by Sir Hilary Brooks, a leading Actor-Manager and Producer of his day. The organization is controlled from London by a committee of leading actors and actresses who attend meetings once a month and make decisions on policy, investments, etc. "The Wings" is comfortable without being luxurious and has a pleasant garden with a view of the river in the distance. The lounge was originally three rooms, hall, dining-room and drawing-room, but these were amalgamated into one when the house was bought and it is now large, airy and cheerful. Up RC *there is a short staircase leading to a small landing with an arch* C *giving access to the upper rooms of the house. Up* LC *are french windows opening on to a flagged terrace which overlooks the garden and the distant Thames.* R *of the staircase is a small hall, at the back of which is a green baize door leading to the kitchen. There is an opening* R *of the hall which goes to the front door and dining-room. A door* C *of the wall* R *leads to the television room. There is a large fireplace* L. *Above this is a door to Miss Archibald's office. Down* R *there is a built-in bureau with a pull-down desk flap and book-shelves over it. In the crook of the stairs is an antiquated but still playable Bechstein Grand piano. The furniture is mixed. There are some fairly good "pieces" here and there, which have been donated at various times, and there are comfortable chairs and a sofa upholstered in faded chintz. The sofa is* C, *angled to face down* L, *and a low coffee-table stands in front of it. In the crook of the piano there is a tub chair. Armchairs are set up* L *and* LC *and there is an easy chair down* L. *A small folding table stands* RC, *with upright chairs* R, L *and above it. An upright chair stands at the bureau, and a butler's tray stands* L *of the hall. An occasional table is above the fireplace and a fire-stool stands at the down-stage end of the hearth. There are central heating radiators down* L *and*

I

on the landing. There is, inevitably, a set of framed playbills of earlier days on the landing wall, and, over the fireplace, dominating the lounge, is a very large but not very good oil painting of Ellen Terry. There is also an impressive bronze bust of the late Sir Hilary Brooks on a pedestal at the top of the stairs. At night, the room is lit by a standard lamp up C and electric candle wall-brackets over the mantelpiece, on the landing and on the wall down R. A small glass chandelier hangs in the hall. The switches are on a pillar R of the staircase, R of the landing arch and below the office door up L. A small fire extinguisher is on the wall L of the landing arch. On the terrace there are three garden chairs.

Before the CURTAIN *rises, the music of "Waiting in the Wings" is heard.*

When the CURTAIN *rises, the music fades. It is a sunny afternoon, just after lunch. The fire is lit, because although it is a summer day it is an English summer day and therefore unpredictable.* BONITA BELGRAVE *and* CORA CLARKE *are seated at the table* RC, *just finishing a game of Canasta.* BONITA, *in her late sixties, is seated above the table. She has reddish blonde hair and is wearing a well-cut but none too new beige jersey dress, two strings of pearls with ear-rings to match and a lucky charm bracelet. She is a gay, bright woman with a strongly developed theatrical sense of humour. She appeared with considerable success in revues and musical comedies during the 1914–18 war, and in the Twenties and Thirties forsook the musical for the legitimate stage. She was never a great star but was popular in supporting parts, worked for ENSA during the second world war and was forced, owing to advancing years and lack of offers, to retire in 1950.* CORA, *who is a year or two older, is very brightly made-up with the rouge on her cheeks placed high. She wears a pink cotton afternoon dress and has a grey cardigan jacket slung over her shoulders. From beneath her coloured turban peep a few very black curls. She has several bead necklaces and a gold chain with a locket.* MAUD MELROSE, *a diminutive soubrette of seventy, is curled up in the upstage corner of the sofa, reading the theatre page of the "Sunday Times". She has rather sparse red hair, a neat blue print dress, enormous horn-rimmed glasses and a vast bag into which she plunges occasionally for her cigarettes and matches. In the years before the first war when she made her début she appeared with success in several musical comedies. Vivacity was her strong suit. She was always an excellent musician and, in her youth, had a piercing soprano voice of startling volume. She appeared sporadically in the period between wars but her life, on the whole, has been a long and fairly fruitless struggle.* MAY DAVENPORT, *aged about seventy-five, is seated bolt upright in the armchair* LC, *working slowly and majestically on an embroidery frame. She was an authentic star in her day and specialized in Shakespeare and the more ponderous Restoration comedies. Her movements are slow and immensely dignified, and she wears a black velvet dress which in earlier years might have been described as a tea-gown. Her hair is coal-black but she has allowed it graciously to go a little grey at the sides. Her discreetly made-up face is still structurally beautiful and she wears a*

narrow black velvet ribbon round her neck. Outside, on the terrace,
Almina Clare *and* Estelle Craven *can be seen through the open
french windows. They are both muffled up against the June weather.*
Estelle *is seated* c *of the terrace. She is aged seventy-four and is white-
haired and permanently wistful. She is knitting.* Almina *is seated* l *of
the terrace. She is aged eighty-five and is immensely fat. She has
dropped off to sleep over the "Sunday Express". They have both been on
the stage all their lives and have played leading parts from time to time
but genuine stardom has eluded them.*

Bonita (*to Cora*) Well, that's that. (*She adds up her score card*)
You owe me two and six.
Cora. You owe me a shilling from last Sunday.
Bonita. In that case you only owe me one and six.
Cora. We'd better hold it over until next time we play.
Bonita. I thought you'd say that.
Cora (*sharply*) Why—may I ask?
Bonita (*sweetly*) Because you always do, dear.
Maud (*looking up from her paper*) I see they're hoping to get
Buck Randy for the *Midnight Matinée* this year.
May. Who in heaven's name is Buck Randy?
Maud. Really, May—you must have heard of Buck Randy.
He's the rage of America.
May. I haven't been to America since nineteen-thirteen. What
does he do?
Maud. He sings, stripped to the waist, to a zither.
May. Why should he be stripped to the waist?
Bonita (*rising and standing behind the sofa*) Because he's sup-
posed to have the most beautiful male body in the world, dear.
He was Mr America of nineteen-fifty-five and nineteen-fifty-six.
(*She crosses to the shelves down* r, *looks at the books and selects one*)
May. Why a zither?
Maud. He accompanies himself on it. Last year one of his
records sold over two million. He has to have police protection
wherever he goes.
May. I'm not surprised.

(Bonita *sits in the desk chair and glances through the book*)

Maud (*looking at her paper*) They say that Carolita Pagadicci is
going to appear, too. She's flying over from Rome specially.
May. Is that the one with the vast bust who came last year and
just stood about?
Cora. I'm sure it's very kind of all of them to take so much
trouble for a bunch of old has-beens like us.
Bonita. Speak for yourself, dear.
Cora. I know they got a lot of publicity out of it but even so
I shouldn't think from their point of view it was worth all the
effort.

MAY. It is always possible, my dear Cora, that just one or two of them might do it from sheer kindness of heart.

CORA. I said it was kind of them to take the trouble, and Bonita flew at me.

BONITA. I didn't fly at you for that. It was because you said we were a bunch of old has-beens.

CORA. We wouldn't be here if we weren't.

MAY. In essence, you are quite right, my dear Cora, but please remember before you say things like that again that it is painful to some of us to be so vulgarly reminded that we are dependent on the charity of our younger colleagues.

CORA. Oh, dear, I'm sure I'm sorry I spoke.

MAY. So are we all, Cora. So are we all.

(DEIRDRE O'MALLEY *stamps in from the television room* R, *leaving the door open. She is a spry, white-haired old woman of eighty-two, attired in dusty black. She speaks with a strong brogue*)

DEIRDRE (*standing above the card table*) I'm telling you all here and now that I would like to take the man who invented tele-vision and strangle the damned life out of him.

BONITA (*rising with her book*) Has it gone wrong again?

DEIRDRE. It has indeed, and for no reason in the world other than pure devilment. (*She crosses above the sofa to* R *of May*) I was sitting there quiet as the grave listening to Father Dugan giving his Sunday afternoon talk when suddenly the damned contrap-tion gets up to its blasphemous tricks, and before me very eyes I see the blessed Father begin to wobble about like a dancing dervish with one side of his saintly face pulled out of shape as though it was made of india-rubber.

BONITA (*moving up* R *towards the hall*) Miss Archie will fix it, dear. I'll go and ask her.

DEIRDRE (*moving towards Bonita*) I'm grateful for the thought but spare yourself the trouble. By the time Miss Archie's fiddled with the damn thing the blessed Father will have finished his talk and be having his tea. (*She goes up the stairs on to the landing*) I'm going up to have me forty winks. It's a dark world we're living in when a bit of soulless machinery can suddenly turn a holy man into a figure of fun.

(DEIRDRE *exits on the landing*)

BONITA (*laughing*) That old girl's wonderful, she really is. (*She moves down* RC) You must have seen her in the old days, May—was she really good? (*She sits on the sofa, at the downstage end*)

(ESTELLE, *on the terrace, puts away her knitting and rises.* ALMINA *wakes and rises*)

MAY (*after a moment's thought*) Good, but unreliable. She's never played a scene the same way twice.

(ESTELLE *and* ALMINA *come into the room*)

ESTELLE (*crossing between May and the sofa to the fireplace*) I'm perished to the bone and it's no good pretending I'm not. (*She puts her knitting bag on the fire-stool and warms her hands at the fire*)

ALMINA (*crossing to* L *of Bonita; quaveringly*) Do you think we shall ever get it?

BONITA. Get what, dear?

ALMINA. The Solarium Lounge.

MAUD (*rising and picking up her bag*) The letter went off to the committee over two weeks ago. (*She moves to the piano, puts her bag on it, then sits on the piano stool*)

BONITA. It probably came up at Friday's meeting.

ALMINA. Even if they say "yes" I shall be dead and gone before they get round to building it. My heart's been pounding again; I hardly slept a wink last night.

(MAUD *starts to strum part of Rachmaninov's Second Piano Concerto in C Minor*)

MAY. You know perfectly well, Almina, that that's only indigestion. Dr Jevons told you so. You eat far too much far too quickly.

ALMINA (*crossing to the easy chair down* L) I like eating. (*She sits*)

ESTELLE (*sitting on the fire-stool*) That east wind comes straight across the valley and cuts you in two.

CORA. The committee could well afford it if they chose. Perry told me so himself.

MAY. As official secretary to the fund he had no right to. That young man talks far too much.

BONITA. Now then, May, you know perfectly well you dote on him—we all do. You gossip away with him for hours whenever you get the chance.

MAY. What nonsense you talk, my dear Bonita.

MAUD (*still playing*) I suppose he'll be down as usual this afternoon.

(CORA *picks up the cards, rises, and pushes her chair into the table*)

CORA. Of course he will, it's Sunday. (*She moves towards the desk*) Also he'll be sure to come today in order to welcome . . .

BONITA (*interrupting; warningly*) Cora!

(CORA *stops.* MAUD *ceases playing.* ESTELLE *and* ALMINA *react*)

CORA (*with a hurried glance at May*) Well, you know what I mean.

(*There is a slightly awkward silence*)

MAY. In order to welcome who?

MAUD (*rising and moving above the sofa; embarrassed*) We've got a new addition to our cosy little family arriving this afternoon.

May. Why wasn't I told? Who is it?

Bonita. Oh, dear, that cat's out of the bag, now, with a vengeance. I suppose we'd better say.

May. What are you all talking about? Why all this mystery?

Bonita. It's Lotta Bainbridge.

May (*stiffening*) Lotta Bainbridge.

Bonita. Yes.

May (*ominously*) Lotta Bainbridge—coming here?

Bonita (*hurriedly*) We all thought—knowing that you and she are not exactly the best of friends—that it would be better not to say anything about it.

May. How long have you known?

Maud. Perry told us last Sunday.

May (*accusingly*) You mean you were all prepared to let me meet her face to face without even warning me? (*She packs her embroidery away in the bag*)

Bonita. Old Dora, her dresser, who's been with her for years, is leaving her to get married, and the maisonnette she had just off the Fulham Road is being pulled down to make way for office buildings . . .

May. I am not in the least interested in where she lives and what is being pulled down. (*She picks up her bag, rises and crosses to the stairs*) I only know that I find your combined conspiracy of silence difficult to forgive.

(Cora *puts the cards on the desk*)

Maud (*putting her hand on May's arm*) It was only that we didn't want to upset you.

May. Do you seriously imagine that it would have upset me less to find her here in this house without being prepared?

(Cora *moves down* r)

Bonita. Don't be angry with us, May. After all, it was a long long time ago, wasn't it? The quarrel, I mean . . .

(Maud *moves to the piano*)

May. There was no quarrel, my dear Bonita. You have been misinformed. (*She goes to the foot of the stairs*)

Bonita (*weakly*) Well, whatever it was then . . .

May. I have not spoken to Lotta Bainbridge for thirty years and I have no intention of doing so now. (*She goes up the stairs to the landing*)

(Estelle *rises*)

Maud (*moving to the foot of the stairs*) Oh, May dear—don't be like that—it's all over and done with.

May (*grandly*) One of you had better explain the situation to her when she arrives. Don't be afraid she won't understand. She'll understand perfectly.

(MAY *exits on the landing. There is an embarrassed silence for a moment or two*)

BONITA. Well, that's that, isn't it?

MAUD (*moving above the card table*) I suppose we ought to have told her really.

BONITA (*moving along the sofa seat to the upstage end*) They'll probably settle down together in time; they can't go on not speaking for ever, but the next few weeks are going to be hell.

(CORA *goes to the desk and collects some patience cards*)

MAUD (*moving behind the sofa*) Who was it that said that there was something beautiful about growing old?

BONITA. Whoever it was I have news for him.

ESTELLE (*picking up her bag and crossing to L of the coffee-table*) Since I've been here I somehow can't remember not being old. (*She puts her bag on the coffee-table*)

BONITA. Perhaps that's something to do with having played character parts for so long.

ESTELLE. I was an *ingénue* for years. I was very pretty and my eyes were enormous. They're quite small now. (*She moves to the armchair LC and sits*)

(CORA *closes the desk*)

MAUD. What started it—the feud between her and May?

BONITA. Come off it, Maudie. You weren't toddling home from school with your pencil box in nineteen-eighteen.

MAUD (*equably*) As a matter of fact that's exactly what I was doing, eight times a week. I was in *Miss Mouse* at the *Adelphi* and I had a number in the last act called "*Don't Play the Fool with a Schoolgirl*". It used to stop the show.

CORA. So far as I can remember it was the notices that stopped the show.

(*The sound of a motor-cycle horn is heard off*)

(*She moves and sits R of the card table*) Here's Perry. He's earlier than usual. (*She lays out the patience cards for a game*)

BONITA (*immediately opening her bag and taking out her compact*) Bless his heart. (*She touches up her face*)

MAUD (*crossing to the french windows*) Don't trouble to do that, dear—it's locking the stable door . . . (*She looks off R*)

BONITA. All right, all right, I know—it's just habit.

ALMINA. He'll tell us whether we're going to get the Solarium Lounge.

CORA. Oh, no, he won't. He'll just say that the committee has it under consideration.

(MAUD *moves and stands up C by the piano*)

BONITA (*replacing the compact in her bag*) In any case we shall
know by his tone whether there's any hope.

CORA. I don't know why you're all working yourselves up
about that damned Solarium. It'll be waste of money even if we
do get it. Just so much more glass for the rain to beat against.

BONITA. That's right, dear—keep us all in hysterics.

(PERRY LASCOE *enters briskly from the hall. He is a nice-looking
young man somewhere between thirty-eight and forty. He is wearing a
sports coat, grey flannel trousers, a highly-coloured pullover and driving
gloves. He carries a crash helmet and goggles. Some years ago he had a
certain success as a musical comedy juvenile but realizing, wisely, that
although he could sing and dance adequately he had little hope of becoming a star, he renounced the shadow for the substance and took on the
job of being secretary to "The Wings" Fund. Most of the inmates
adore him because he jokes with them and jollies them along and is
fundamentally kind*)

PERRY (*standing above the card table*) Hullo, everybody.

LADIES (*ad lib.*) Hullo, Perry.

PERRY. My dears, I'm in trouble.

MAUD (*moving to L of Perry*) What sort of trouble?

PERRY. I knocked over a milk cart in Maidenhead. Fortunately they were mostly empties. The milkman was livid. (*He looks
around*) Where's old May? (*He puts his helmet and goggles on the chair
above the card table*)

BONITA. Upstairs.

PERRY. Good.

BONITA. Not so good. She knows.

PERRY (*removing his gloves and putting them with his helmet*) Oh,
Lord! Who told her?

MAUD. We all did—we had to.

PERRY. Well, maybe it's all for the best.

BONITA. It isn't. She's hopping mad.

PERRY. Oh, poor Lotta. She's got enough to put up with
without this.

CORA. When's she arriving?

PERRY. Any minute now. (*He crosses to R of Estelle*) Billy
Musgrove lent her his car and Dora's bringing her down with
all her bits and pieces. (*He kisses Estelle*)

MAUD. Have you seen her?

PERRY. Yes—last week. I went along to her flat and had tea
with her and made all the final arrangements.

BONITA. How did she look?

PERRY. Sort of miserable, but she tried not to show it.

(MAUD *moves to the downstage end of the sofa and sits*)

I don't think she minds about the flat so much, it's Dora leaving her that's really got her down. (*He crosses to Almina and kisses her*) Where's the Colonel?

CORA. In her office, deciding whether we're going to have Shepherd's Pie or Macaroni Cheese for supper, I expect.

ALMINA. We had Macaroni Cheese last night and it nearly killed me.

(SYLVIA ARCHIBALD, *known as* MISS ARCHIE, *enters from her office up* L. *She is the resident superintendent of "The Wings". She is a woman of about fifty. Her gruff and rather masculine manner conceals a vulnerable heart and an amiable disposition. She is fairly popular with the inmates although at moments she is a trifle overbearing. Her build is on the bulky side, which does not prevent her from wearing corduroy trousers and rather tight woollen sweaters. She worked diligently for ENSA during World War Two and retired at the end of it with the rank of Colonel. This, incidentally, is her greatest pride*)

MISS ARCHIE (*crossing to* L *of the coffee-table*) There you are, Perry.

PERRY. Hullo, ducks.

MISS ARCHIE. I thought I heard the old bike.

PERRY. The old bike's older than ever since the last half hour. She grazed her knees against a milk cart.

MISS ARCHIE (*whistling*) Good Lord! That means ten days confined to barracks for you, my lad. (*She collects the newspapers from the coffee-table*)

PERRY. I love to hear you talk like that, Archie. It reminds me of my Uncle Edgar.

MISS ARCHIE. Never mind about your Uncle Edgar now, Perry. What time is Lotta Bainbridge arriving?

PERRY. Any moment now. (*He sits on the fire-stool*) She's coming down in Billy Musgrove's car.

MISS ARCHIE. Nobody ever tells me anything. (*She puts the newspapers on the piano*) Has Osgood been yet?

BONITA. No. He's late.

PERRY. How *is* poor old Martha?

MISS ARCHIE. She was a bit under the weather on Friday and yesterday, but she always perks up on Sundays. (*She crosses to the card table, picks up the ashtray and empties it in the waste-paper basket below the desk*)

ESTELLE. Old Osgood must be seventy if he's a day.

MAUD. Were they ever lovers, do you think? I mean, in the old days.

(MISS ARCHIE *closes the door of the television room, then replaces the ashtray on the card table*)

PERRY (*laughing*) Good heavens, no! He's twenty-five years younger than she is, to start with. No, no, it's just star-worship, a sort of obsession. He used to wait outside stage doors for her when she was in her heyday and he was only a young boy. Rain or shine there he'd be with his bunch of violets.

MAUD. He still brings her violets.

PERRY. I know. It really is rather sweet, isn't it?

CORA. I was in the last play she ever did. We all loathed her.

(*The front-door bell rings*)

MISS ARCHIE. There he is now, I expect. I'll answer her. Doreen's gone to the village.

(MISS ARCHIE *exits in the hall to* R)

PERRY. Is Doreen working out all right?

CORA. She has adenoids and no time sense——

(*The front door is heard to slam*)

—but she's better than that awful Gladys.

PERRY. I rather liked Gladys, she was like a bad character performance in Act Three.

(MISS ARCHIE *enters from the hall.*
      OSGOOD MEEKER *follows her on. He is an elderly, bald-headed man, nattily dressed and rather dim. He carries a bunch of violets.*
PERRY *rises*)

OSGOOD (*moving behind the sofa; with a courtly manner*) Good afternoon, ladies.

(MISS ARCHIE *stands at the foot of the stairs*)

BONITA. Hullo, Osgood. How are you?

OSGOOD. Fine, thank you, my dear. A little twinge every now and then, you know, but apart from that, fit as a fiddle.

MISS ARCHIE (*going on to the landing*) I'll take you up.

OSGOOD (*following Miss Archie on to the landing*) No, please don't trouble, Miss Archie. I know the way. She is expecting me, isn't she?

(PERRY *resumes his seat*)

MISS ARCHIE. Yes, Mr Meeker—she's always expecting you.

OSGOOD. Has she been—er—happier this last week?

MISS ARCHIE. Oh, yes. She was a little low on Friday and yesterday, but nothing to worry about.

OSGOOD (*crossing to* L *of Miss Archie on the landing*) I'll go on up, then.

MISS ARCHIE. I'll have a cup of tea for you when you come down.

OSGOOD. Thank you, my dear, thank you. That will be delightful.

(OSGOOD *exits on the landing*)

Maud. Do you think she recognizes him?

Miss Archie. Oh, yes. He's never caught her on one of her bad days. She gets quite gay with him sometimes and tells him risky stories about the past—her memory's fantastic, at least for things that happened a long while ago.

Perry. That's quite usual, isn't it? I mean when people get old they can recall, say, Queen Victoria's Jubilee, and not be able to remember what happened last week.

Cora. Nothing did.

Estelle. One thing I can remember and that is that we wrote a round robin to the committee two weeks ago about having a Solarium Lounge so that we could enjoy the sun without being frozen to death. (*To Perry*) Did they read it?

Perry. Yes. It came up at Friday's meeting.

Bonita. What did they say?

Perry. They said they'd consider it.

Cora. There now—what did I tell you!

(Miss Archie *comes down the stairs and stands* r *of Estelle*)

Estelle. Is there any hope, do you think?

Perry (*rising and kneeling beside Estelle*) Of course there is. We must always look on the bright side.

Cora (*rising and moving behind the sofa*) None of that bedside manner stuff, Perry. You don't think they're going to let us have it, do you?

Perry (*rising*) I tell you they said they'd consider it—I really don't know.

Bonita. You could tell from the way they discussed it which way the wind was blowing, couldn't you?

Cora. Didn't anyone even suggest sending for an estimate?

Perry (*unhappily*) I gave them an estimate—with the letter.

Cora. How do you mean?

Perry. Hodges and Creal did it for me.

(Miss Archie *moves to the french windows and looks out*)

Miss Archie and I measured the whole terrace last Sunday evening, after you'd all gone to bed.

Bonita. I thought I heard someone scuffling about under my window. I thought it was burglars.

Cora. No burglar'd be fool enough to prowl round this house.

Miss Archie (*turning and moving* c) How much was the estimate? How much did Hodges and Creal say it would cost?

Perry. Two thousand five hundred.

Bonita. God Almighty, what are they planning to build it of —uranium?

Miss Archie. It's the frontage, I expect. It's a very wide frontage, and glass costs an awful lot.

Bonita. Were any of the committee in favour of it?

PERRY (*flatly*) One or two, but not the majority.

CORA. Do you mean to say the Fund couldn't afford it—even after poor Maurice's legacy?

PERRY. That's already been invested.

CORA. What did Boodie Nethersole say?

PERRY. She was not in favour of it.

CORA. Oh, she wasn't, wasn't she?

MISS ARCHIE (*warningly*) Look here, Perry my lad, you know you're not supposed to discuss the committee.

BONITA (*irritably*) Oh, go and form fours for a minute, dear——

(MISS ARCHIE *moves to the french windows*)

—this is important to all of us.

CORA. Boodie Nethersole indeed! I'd like to strangle her.

BONITA. So would I if I could find her neck.

MISS ARCHIE. I say—steady.

CORA (*moving to the chair* R *of the card table*) She has no right to be on the committee, anyhow; she can't act her way out of a paper bag and never could. (*She sits and plays patience*)

PERRY. She's had four whacking successes in the last five years.

BONITA. What did she say exactly?

(PERRY *moves behind Estelle*)

PERRY (*after a pause*) I really can't say any more. She was just a bit more bossy about it than the others.

BONITA. You mean she swung them round against the idea?

PERRY. Yes—I suppose so.

ESTELLE. Perhaps it was too much to ask. The home is very comfortable on the whole, but it would have been nice to enjoy the sun when it comes out without having to face that awful East wind.

(PERRY *puts his arms around Estelle, over the back of the chair*)

PERRY. I promise I'll bring it up again at the next meeting, when there aren't quite so many of them there.

ESTELLE (*rising and moving to* L *of the coffee-table*) I feel it's all my fault really for having suggested it in the first place. Now you're all disappointed and I'm to blame. (*She picks up her bag, near to tears*)

BONITA. Cheer up, dear—it doesn't matter all that much.

ESTELLE (*moving to the stairs*) I was so looking forward to it—we all were—it would have been so lovely. (*She weeps and turns to go up the stairs*)

(PERRY *moves quickly to* L *of the banisters and leans over them to Estelle*)

PERRY. Don't cry, my old duck egg—I'll swing it somehow, you see if I don't. I'll get another estimate from another firm, one that isn't quite so posh as Hodges and Creal, and we'll knock a bit off here and bit off there and I'll get the committee to agree if it's the last thing I do.

(ESTELLE, *weeping, goes up the stairs and exits on the landing.* BONITA *rises and throws her book on to the coffee-table*)

BONITA (*crossing to the fireplace*) That Boodie Nethersole! I'll have a few words to say to her the next time she comes bouncing down here in her bloody Bentley.
CORA (*rising and crossing to* C) Oh, for Heaven's sake let's change the subject. As Bonita said, it doesn't matter all that much anyhow. A little while ago we'd none of us even heard of a Solarium —we've all got one foot in the grave, anyway.
BONITA. Excuse me while I slip into my shroud.

(*The front-door bell rings*)

PERRY. That'll be Lotta Bainbridge, I expect.
MISS ARCHIE (*crossing to the card table*) Be a good chap, Perry, and yell for Ted to take up the bags—he's in the kitchen.

(MAUD *rises and tidies the sofa cushions*)

PERRY. Right.

(PERRY *exits to the kitchen*)

MISS ARCHIE (*briskly*) I'll go to the door. (*She moves to the hall*) I hate welcoming new arrivals, they always look sort of lost.

(MISS ARCHIE *exits* R *in the hall.* MAUD *goes to the card table, packs up the cards, puts them in the desk, then stands down* R. ALMINA *rises and tidies herself*)

CORA. It's nothing to the way they look after they've been here a few months.
BONITA. Why do you say that, Cora, you know you don't really mean it.
CORA. Perhaps I was trying to be funny.
MISS ARCHIE (*off*) Come along—this way, Miss Bainbridge.

(MISS ARCHIE *enters from the hall and stands by the door* R. LOTTA BAINBRIDGE *and* DORA, *her maid, follow Miss Archie on.* LOTTA *is a well-preserved woman in her early seventies. Her hair, which was once blonde, is now ash-coloured. She wears a small hat and a dust-coat over a plain but well-cut dress. She is well made-up and calmly cheerful. She stands at the foot of the stairs.* DORA, *who is carrying a suitcase, stands in the hall. She is in her forties and is fat and morose. She has obviously been crying*)

LOTTA (*with a smile*) Well, this is all very exciting—rather like going to a new school—(*she sees Cora*) except of course that at a new school one doesn't meet old friends. (*She crosses to* C) Cora!

(CORA *meets Lotta* C. MISS ARCHIE *moves to* MAUD *and sends her to greet Lotta*)

I haven't seen you for years. (*She kisses Cora*)
    CORA. No. (*She stands above the chair* LC)
    MAUD (*crossing to* R *of Lotta*) How do you do, Miss Bainbridge?
    LOTTA. Miss Melrose? (*She shakes hands with Maud*)
    MAUD. Yes.

(DORA *comes in from the hall and puts the case down by the door* R)

    LOTTA. We're not exactly old friends but I have admired you so often—I remember you years ago singing a most enchanting song dressed as a schoolgirl—I've forgotten the name of the play . . .
    MAUD. It was "*Miss Mouse*" at the *Adelphi*.
    LOTTA. *Miss Mouse*—of course it was.

(MAUD *moves down* R)

(*She crosses to Bonita*) You're Bonita Belgrave, aren't you? I'd recognize you anywhere. I knew you were here because we have a great friend in common—Lucas Bradshaw.
    BONITA. Luke Bradshaw! I didn't know he was still alive. How is the old soak?
    LOTTA. Still soaking, I'm afraid, but only every now and then. He comes to see me sometimes in his more lucid moments and we reminisce about the good old days.
    CORA. A lot of that goes on here.
    LOTTA. Between ourselves, you know, I'm really getting a bit tired of the good old days—but I suppose it is fun, once in a while, to wander back for a little.
    MISS ARCHIE (*crossing below the sofa*) You know Almina Clare.
    LOTTA. Of course I do.

(ALMINA *moves to Lotta*)

Almina! (*She kisses her*)

(PERRY *enters from the kitchen and greets* DORA, *who is on the verge of tears*)

You really are very naughty to have put on so much weight. You used to be thin as a rail.
    ALMINA. I like eating and there's no need to diet any more.
    LOTTA. No, I suppose there isn't really.
    PERRY (*crossing to* R *of Lotta*) Welcome to St Trinians, Miss Bainbridge.

(ALMINA *moves to the easy chair down* L *and sits*)

    LOTTA. Why, Mr Lascoe. (*She shakes hands with Perry*) I had no idea you would be here to greet me—how very nice. (*She crosses to the foot of the stairs and looks at the bust*) I remember that bust of Hilary. He was sitting for it when we were playing in *Brief Candles*. (*She moves to Dora and leads her* C) This is my beloved Dora. She's going to be married in a month's time. We don't talk about being separated much because we burst into tears. Why don't you go upstairs, Dora, and do just a little unpacking for me, as a sort of final gesture. Would you be very kind and show her where my room is, Miss Archibald?

MISS ARCHIE (*picking up Lotta's case and moving to the stairs*) Certainly. Follow me, Dora.

(MISS ARCHIE *goes up the stairs and exits on the landing.*
    DORA *slowly follows her off*)

PERRY (*taking Lotta's cloak*) May I?
LOTTA. Oh, thank you very much.

(PERRY *puts the cloak on the chair up* L)

(*She sits on the sofa*) Oh, dear, I really felt quite nervous when I came in, like a first night.

(PERRY *moves to the upstage end of the sofa*)

But I feel better now. Sarita Myrtle's here, isn't she?
PERRY. Yes, but she's a bit round the bend, as you probably know.
LOTTA (*removing her gloves*) Poor Sarita, she was always vague, even in the old days.
CORA. May Davenport is here, too.
LOTTA. Yes. Yes, I know she is. (*She looks up at the picture over the fireplace*) I wonder who painted that picture of dear Ellen Terry. It really isn't very good, is it? But even flat painting can't quite subdue her radiance, can it?
BONITA (*suddenly crossing to Lotta*) It's awfully nice to have you here, Miss Bainbridge—we're all tremendously thrilled. (*She kisses Lotta*)

(CORA *sits on the left arm of the chair* LC)

LOTTA (*nearly undone for a moment*) Thank you, dear—thank you very much.
PERRY (*to cover a little silence*) You'll love Miss Archie when you get to know her.
LOTTA. I'm sure I shall.
PERRY (*crossing to the fireplace*) She slips into uniform at the drop of a hat.

(LOTTA *removes her hat and puts it with her gloves on the seat beside her*)

She retired from ENSA at the end of the war with the rank of full colonel. But underneath that gruff exterior there beats a heart of pure gold.

LOTTA. I suppose I really should go upstairs and help Dora and see my room, but I don't feel I want to just yet. I shall be seeing quite enough of it in the years to come.

MAUD (*moving behind the sofa*) It's one of the best ones; it looks out over the kitchen garden.

LOTTA (*wryly*) How lovely!

BONITA. Don't dread it, please don't dread any of it; it's not nearly as bad as you think—really it isn't.

LOTTA. I've tried not to think very much during the last few weeks. It seemed more sensible. I'm very fortunate to have this place to come to. I suppose we all are, really.

CORA. That's a matter of opinion.

BONITA. Oh, shut up, Cora.

LOTTA. I remember driving down here with Hilary years ago a few months after he had opened it. It was a lovely summer day —we had tea in the garden. Little did I think then that one day I should be coming here to live.

BONITA. It's quite a pleasant life really. We have television and sometimes we go to the movies in Maidenhead and have tea at the Picture House café—the bus stop is only five minutes' walk.

LOTTA (*absently*) I must catch up on my movies—I've been shamefully neglectful lately.

BONITA. Why don't you sit here quietly for a little and relax and sort of get accustomed to the atmosphere? (*She picks up her book from the coffee-table and crosses below the card table*) It's about time for our afternoon snooze, anyhow. Are you coming up, Cora?

CORA (*reluctantly*) Yes, I suppose so. (*She rises*)

LOTTA (*with an effort*) You all know, don't you, that May Davenport and I have not been on speaking terms for many many years?

CORA. Yes—yes, we do.

BONITA. Don't worry—it'll all work out in the long run.

LOTTA. The situation is not without humour. It is certainly ironic that fate should arrange so neatly for May and me to end our days under the same roof. Personally I can't help seeing the funny side of it, but I doubt if May does.

BONITA. She doesn't, not at the moment, but she probably will in time.

LOTTA. A sense of humour was never one of her outstanding characteristics.

MAUD. She sometimes says awfully funny things.

LOTTA. She always did, but generally unintentionally. All I want to explain to you is that I am fully armed with olive branches. I couldn't bear to think that my coming here was in any way an embarrassment to you. I shall do my best, but please don't blame me too much if I fail. May is fairly implacable.

CORA (*moving* C) I suppose it would be too much to ask what caused the feud in the first place.

LOTTA. Yes, Cora, it would. In any case it would be redundant because I am well aware that you know the whole story.
BONITA. If ever I've heard a cue for exit, Cora, that's it. Come on up.
ALMINA (*heaving herself up from her chair with an effort*) Oh, dear.
PERRY (*moving to Almina and helping her*) Come on, love—you can make it if you don't weaken. (*He leads Almina to the stairs*)

(ALMINA *goes slowly up the stairs and exits on the landing.*
PERRY *exits to the hall.* CORA *goes to the piano and gets a newspaper.* BONITA *moves to the book-shelves and chooses another book*)

MAUD. See you later, Miss Bainbridge. (*She moves up* RC)
LOTTA. *Au revoir*, Miss Mouse.
MAUD (*laughing*) Oh, it wasn't me that was "Miss Mouse"—I was only the soubrette. It was poor Dolly Drexell—actually it was the last thing she did before she went off her rocker—you remember her, don't you?

(CORA *and* BONITA *move to the foot of the stairs*)

LOTTA. Vaguely.
MAUD (*crossing to the piano*) China blue eyes and no middle register. (*She collects her bag*)
BONITA (*going up the stairs*) We mustn't forget to ask Miss Archie to fix the television before tonight.

(CORA *and* MAUD *follow Bonita up the stairs.*
PERRY *enters from the hall*)

There's a new quiz game.
CORA. I hate quiz games.
BONITA. You never actually *played* "*Rebecca of Sunnybrook Farm*", did you, dear?

(BONITA, MAUD *and* CORA *exit on the landing*)

PERRY (*moving above the sofa*) Would you really like to be left alone for a bit?
LOTTA. No. I'm quite happy. Dora will be down in a minute anyhow, then, if you don't mind I should like you to leave us—it will be a rather painful good-bye scene I'm afraid. She's been working up for it all day.
PERRY (*offering his cigarette case*) Cigarette?
LOTTA. Thank you. (*She takes a cigarette*)

(PERRY *lights Lotta's cigarette, draws the chair* LC *nearer to her and sits*)

PERRY. Is Billy's car taking her back to London?
LOTTA. Yes. It was dear of him to lend it to me. She'll go back to the flat and do all the final tidying up. Poor old Dora. I shall miss her dreadfully.

PERRY. Have you seen him—the husband to be?

LOTTA. Yes, once—she brought him to tea. He seemed nice enough, massive, but with a very small head.

PERRY. Does he really love her?

LOTTA. I couldn't really tell. He stared at her fixedly all the time, if that is anything to go by. I expect she'll miss me a lot at first, but she'll soon get over it.

PERRY. Everybody gets over everything in time.

LOTTA (with a smile) I do so hope you're right.

PERRY. You'll soon get to like it here. I'm sure you will.

LOTTA. I'm sure I shall, too.

PERRY. If there's anything that really upsets you, anything that you really hate, do let me know privately and, if necessary, I can tactfully bring it up before the committee.

LOTTA. Thank you, you're very kind. I don't suppose there will be.

PERRY. Well, just remember—if you need me I'll be down like a flash.

LOTTA. You gave up the theatre very young, didn't you?

PERRY. Yes, six years ago, when I was thirty-three.

LOTTA. Why?

PERRY. I started out believing that I was going to be a star and then I suddenly realized that I wasn't.

LOTTA. I see. (She pauses) Do you regret it?

PERRY. No, not really. Every now and then I get a pang or two when I see some young man prancing about the stage and I think to myself "I could have done that better", but really, deep down, I'm not altogether sure that I could have.

LOTTA. And you like this job? You like having to cope with all these old shadows?

PERRY. It's a fixed salary to start with, so mum's taken care of, and I love the—the old shadows.

(MISS ARCHIE enters briskly down the stairs)

The committee gets me down a bit sometimes, but you can't have everything.

MISS ARCHIE (standing above the sofa) Dora's nearly finished, Miss Bainbridge. She'll be down in a minute. Unless you'd care to go up?

LOTTA. No. I'd rather wait here, I think.

MISS ARCHIE (to Perry) Buzz off for a minute, Perry, there's a good chap. I'd like to have a little talk with Miss Bainbridge.

PERRY (rising and replacing the chair LC) Where shall I buzz to?

MISS ARCHIE. Go and look at the telly.

PERRY. I can't, it's bust.

MISS ARCHIE. I bet that's old Deirdre, she's always losing her temper and bashing it with her stick. I'll deal with it later.

PERRY. I'll brave the East wind in the garden.

MISS ARCHIE. Good.

PERRY. Good-bye for the moment, Miss Bainbridge.

LOTTA. Thank you—thank you for being so considerate and kind.

(PERRY *exits by the french windows*)

MISS ARCHIE. Good value that lad. We get on like a house on fire.

LOTTA. I'm glad. I'm sure it's awfully important that you should.

MISS ARCHIE (*moving to the coffee-table*) Do you mind if I smoke? (*She takes a cigarette from the box on the coffee-table*)

LOTTA. No, of course not.

MISS ARCHIE (*crossing to the fireplace*) Before he came we had a woman secretary, nearly drove me round the bend I can tell you. Always in a frizz about something and absolutely terrified of the committee. I used to say to her over and over again, "Listen, old girl—a committee's something you've got to stand up to, and, what's more, they're grateful to you for it in the long run. They don't know what they're talking about half the time, anyhow." You know what actors and actresses are like on a committee? (*She takes a box of matches from the mantelpiece and lights her cigarette*)

LOTTA. Yes, indeed. I served on this committee myself for three years in the thirties.

MISS ARCHIE. Oh, Lord! I certainly put my neck out that time, didn't I?

LOTTA. Not at all. I agree with you on the whole. I wish now that I had taken a little more trouble. I'm sure we all tried to visualize it all from the point of view of the inmates themselves, but I'm not sure that we succeeded.

MISS ARCHIE. It's running pretty smoothly now, thank the Lord. Perry is liaison officer between the committee and me—we have our ups and downs occasionally, of course, but most of the time we manage to keep on an even keel. Now then, in regard to rules and regulations . . . (*She moves the fire-stool LC and sits*)

LOTTA (*ruefully*) Oh, dear!

MISS ARCHIE. Don't be alarmed, there aren't many restrictions.

LOTTA (*ironically*) Are we allowed out alone?

MISS ARCHIE. Good Lord, yes. You can go anywhere you like.

LOTTA. Not quite, I'm afraid.

MISS ARCHIE. One rule we're very firm about is—no pets.

LOTTA. Yes, I know. Mr Lascoe explained that to me last week. I had my little dog put to sleep the day before yesterday. I bought him at the Army and Navy Stores nine years ago when he was a tiny puppy. He was very devoted to me and I don't think he would have been happy with anyone else.

MISS ARCHIE. I say, I'm most awfully sorry—that's damned hard luck.

LOTTA (*rising*) Please don't sympathize with me about it. (*She picks up her bag and gloves and moves down* R) It's the only thing, among my present rather dismal circumstances, that is liable to break me down.

(DORA *enters slowly down the stairs*)

MISS ARCHIE. I quite understand.

LOTTA. Here comes Dora. (*She puts her bag and gloves on the table*) I wonder if you would be very kind and leave us alone for a few minutes; she has to get back to London.

(MISS ARCHIE *rises.* DORA *puts her bag on the tub chair*)

You can brief me about the rest of the rules and regulations later on.

(MISS ARCHIE *replaces the stool* L *and moves up* LC)

I expect there'll be lots of time.

MISS ARCHIE. Of course. Well, cheerio for the moment. I'll be in my office if you want me.

(MISS ARCHIE *nods cheerfully to Dora and exits up* L. LOTTA *goes to Dora and takes her hand*)

LOTTA (*after a brief pause*) How's the room, Dora?

DORA. Quite nice, dear. It's a bit chintzy but there's a pretty view and it is quiet.

LOTTA (*moving to the sofa*) Where is it? (*She sits on the sofa at the upstage end*)

DORA. Second door to the right along the passage. (*She moves to the stairs*) Do you want to come up now?

LOTTA. No. I'll save it until after you've gone.

DORA (*moving behind the sofa; near to tears*) I can't go away and leave you here, dear—I thought I could but I can't.

LOTTA. Don't talk nonsense, Dora. Of course you can. You must. There's nothing else to be done, anyhow.

(DORA *crosses to* L *of Lotta*)

You know that as well as I do.

DORA (*sobbing*) I can't bear it—after all these years—I just can't bear it.

LOTTA (*taking Dora's hand*) Pull yourself together, my dear, for my sake as well as for your own.

DORA. I'll tell Frank he'd better go off and marry someone else, I swear to God I will.

(LOTTA *releases Dora's hand*)

You and me will find a flat somewhere and go along as we always have—I can't go off and leave you in a sort of workhouse. (*She kneels at Lotta's feet, with her arms around Lotta's waist and her head in her lap*)

Lotta (*smiling*) It isn't a workhouse, Dora. It's a very smart home for retired actresses. And in a few days, when the first strangeness has worn off, I'm quite sure I shall be far happier here and far less lonely than I should be in a flat. (*She raises Dora by the shoulders*)˙ Oh, my dear, you have many more years than I have to live and enjoy. For goodness' sake see to it that you enjoy them. You have Frank and those two nice step-daughters to look after——

(Dora *drops her head into Lotta's lap and weeps*)

—and you couldn't have stayed with me much longer, anyhow, because I couldn't afford it. And if I died I should have nothing to leave you and you'd be alone—I couldn't bear the thought of that. We've talked about this over and over again. (*She holds Dora's face*) Please, please, dear Dora, don't cry any more. It isn't nearly so bad as it looks.

(Dora *rises*)

(*She rises and leads Dora up* c) You've promised, remember, to come down and see me next Sunday fortnight.

Dora (*with an effort*) Yes—yes, I know.

Lotta. I shall look forward to it, and I shall write to you first thing tomorrow, and let you know how my first meeting with May went off.

Dora. Horrible old cat.

Lotta. Now, now, now—she may have mellowed with the years.

Dora (*picking up her bag*) I'll give her "mellow" if I get within spitting distance of her.

Lotta (*embracing her*) Dora—darling old Dora. I want you now this very minute to go out of the house, get into the car and drive away. (*She leads Dora towards the hall*) Don't let's either of us say another word. I'm beginning to feel a little tremulous myself. Please. (*She embraces Dora*) Please—dearest old friend—away with you. (*She gives her a little push*)

(Dora, *weeping, goes into the hall*)

Dora. I've put the snapshot of Poochie on the mantelpiece— the one with the ball in his mouth.

Lotta (*with a break in her voice*) Thank you, Dora—thank you.

Dora *exits* r *in the hall.* Lotta, *left alone, bites her lip in a determined effort to control her tears. She goes to the card table, picks up her bag and gloves, collects her hat and cloak, looks slowly round the room, gazes up at the portrait over the mantelpiece for a moment, then exits slowly up the stairs as—*

the Curtain *falls*

SCENE 2

SCENE—*The same. 3 a.m. on a Monday morning, a month later.*

Before the CURTAIN *rises, the music of "Waiting in the Wings" is heard.*

When the CURTAIN *rises, the music fades. The windows and curtains are closed. The hall light, the standard lamp and the landing wall-bracket are lit. There is a small fire in the grate.* DOREEN *enters from the kitchen carrying a tray with two plates of sandwiches. She is a rather untidy girl of about twenty-three. She goes to the coffee-table and puts the plates on it, then moves to the foot of the stairs.* MISS ARCHIE *enters on the landing. She is wearing a man's khaki-coloured dressing-gown and rather old fur-lined slippers. She pauses and looks at her watch.*

MISS ARCHIE. They ought to be here soon. Is the soup on?

DOREEN. Yes, Miss Archibald.

MISS ARCHIE (*glancing off*) I just took a look at the two old ladies—they're both asleep. (*She comes down the stairs and stands* C) I hope the others won't disturb them. You'd better have a kettle going, too, some of them will probably want tea.

DOREEN (*moving to* R *of the stairs; yawning*) Yes, Miss Archibald. (*She switches on the wall-bracket* R)

MISS ARCHIE. Sorry to keep you up, Doreen. You can have an extra hour in the morning. They'll all be kipping late after tonight. (*She goes to the french windows, draws aside the curtains and peers out into the darkness*) Still raining, damn it. That means that the roads will be greasy and Baxter will have to drive slowly.

DOREEN (*moving* C) The show's tomorrow, isn't it, Miss Archibald?

MISS ARCHIE. Yes. (*She glances at her watch*) Tonight, really. (*She moves to the door* L) It's three o'clock in the morning. (*She switches on the wall-brackets* L)

DOREEN. Is it true that Buck Randy's in it?

MISS ARCHIE (*moving to the fireplace*) Yes, I think so.

DOREEN (*ecstatically*) Coo, he's smashing!

MISS ARCHIE. You've never seen him, have you?

DOREEN. He was on the telly last week. The man made him take off his shirt and sing a song—it was lovely.

(SARITA MYRTLE *enters on the landing. She is a wispy old lady in the late seventies. She wears a dressing-gown and slippers*)

MISS ARCHIE (*seeing Sarita*) Miss Myrtle! I thought you were asleep.

SARITA. Everyone has forgotten me. The house is empty and I'm left alone—except for Martha Carrington.

MISS ARCHIE (*anxiously*) You didn't wake her, did you?

SARITA (*giggling*) No. I passed her door on tiptoe. She was snoring.

(Doreen *moves to* r *of the stairs*)

Miss Archie (*moving up* c) Miss Myrtle, you're really very naughty. You ought to be in bed, you know you ought.

Sarita. Please let me come down to the fire, my room is so cold. (*She moves to the top of the stairs*)

Miss Archie. You know that's not true, dear—it's right next to the airing cupboard.

Sarita (*coming slowly down the stairs*) "Out damned spot! Out, I say!"

(Doreen, *fascinated, backs* r)

"One, two: why then, 'tis time to do 't." (*She reaches the foot of the stairs*)

(Doreen *retreats down* r)

Miss Archie (*moving to Sarita; firmly*) You must *not* quote *Macbeth* in this house, Miss Myrtle. You know how it upsets everybody.

Sarita (*with a slight giggle*) There isn't anybody to upset—all the rooms on the landing are "empty, vast and wandering air" —perhaps it is the end of the world. (*She catches sight of the sandwiches*) Good heavens! Sandwiches! (*She moves to the coffee-table*) Whoever thought of sandwiches on the day of judgement.

Miss Archie (*moving to* r *of Sarita*) It isn't the day of judgement, old dear, it's three o'clock on Monday morning, and you must go back to bed.

Sarita. But why the sandwiches?

Miss Archie (*patiently*) They're for the others when they come back from the rehearsal at the *Palladium*. You went with them last year, don't you remember?

Sarita. Why didn't I go this year?

Miss Archie. Because Dr Jevons said it would be bad for you. He said your heart wasn't up to it.

Sarita. There isn't anything wrong with my heart. It's my head that betrays me. It's so noisy. The island is full of noises. My head is an island. An island is a piece of land entirely surrounded by water. Please, may I have a glass of water?

Miss Archie (*to Doreen*) Run into the kitchen and get her one, there's a good girl.

Doreen (*awe-stricken*) Oooh, dear!

(Doreen *runs off to the kitchen*)

Miss Archie. Now, Miss Myrtle, you go back to bed and I'll bring the water up to you.

Sarita. Who is that girl who runs about?

Miss Archie. You know Doreen, dear. She brings you your breakfast every morning.

SARITA (*moving to the fireplace*) "Doreen" is a very common name, don't you think?

MISS ARCHIE. Well, that's not her fault.

SARITA. All names ending in "een" are common—Doreen—Maureen—Noreen . . .

MISS ARCHIE (*humouring her*) Eileen—Kathleen—they're all right, aren't they?

SARITA. Eileen and Kathleen who?

(DOREEN *enters from the kitchen with a glass of water*)

DOREEN (*crossing to Sarita*) Here you are, Miss Myrtle.

SARITA. What is this for?

MISS ARCHIE. You asked for a glass of water.

SARITA (*graciously accepting the glass*) Thank you, my dear child —thank you very much. I hope you enjoyed the performance.

DOREEN (*to Miss Archie; startled*) What does she mean?

MISS ARCHIE. Never mind—just say "yes", it saves time.

DOREEN. Yes, Miss Myrtle.

SARITA. I am afraid it was a rather dull matinée audience— (*she crosses to the sofa*) it was the boat race, I expect—their minds were divided.

MISS ARCHIE. Take her back to bed, Doreen.

SARITA (*taking a sandwich*) I don't care for ham sandwiches as a rule but tonight I'm hungry as a hunter.

(*The sound of a motor horn is heard off.* SARITA *sits on the sofa at the upstage end*)

MISS ARCHIE. Here they are. Run and open the door, Doreen.

DOREEN. Yes, Miss Archibald.

(DOREEN *exits* R *in the hall*)

MISS ARCHIE (*taking the glass from Sarita*) You really must go back to bed, Miss Myrtle. Whatever would Dr Jevons say if he found you wandering about the house in the middle of the night in your dressing-gown?

SARITA (*suddenly bursting into tears*) Please don't send me back to bed—it's so lonely and cold upstairs with all those empty rooms —please let me stay here—please, please, please . . .

MISS ARCHIE (*distracted*) There, there, old dear, there's nothing to cry about. (*She puts her arm rather clumsily around Sarita*) All right, you can stay down here, if you really want to, but do try not to get over-excited. (*She moves down* RC)

SARITA (*cheering up*) I don't know who you are, but you smell like horses.

(ESTELLE, BONITA, MAY, CORA, DEIRDRE *and* ALMINA *enter from the hall. They wear outdoor clothes, headscarves, gloves, etc.*)

ESTELLE (*crossing to the fire-stool*) It's raining cats and dogs. I thought we'd never get here.

BONITA (*moving above the sofa*) Good God, what's Sarita doing? Oughtn't she to be in bed?

(MAY *and* CORA *cross to* C. DEIRDRE *moves down* R)

MISS ARCHIE (*putting the glass on the card table; helplessly*) She woke up and came down only a few minutes ago——

(MAY *and* CORA *pause on seeing* SARITA *who graciously holds out her hand to May*)

—and I can't get her back.

(DOREEN *enters the hall from* R. BONITA *leans over the back of the sofa and taps Sarita's shoulder*)

BONITA. Hullo, dear—I haven't seen you for a long time.

SARITA (*munching her sandwich*) I've been away on tour.

(MAY *sits in the armchair* LC. ESTELLE *sits on the fire-stool.* BONITA *moves and sits on the sofa at the downstage end.* DEIRDRE *sits on the chair below the card table.* CORA *crosses to the easy chair down* L.

ALMINA *stands above the coffee-table. They all remove their gloves, scarves, etc., when they settle themselves in their chairs*)

MISS ARCHIE (*moving up* R *to Doreen*) You can bring in the soup now, Doreen.

DOREEN. O.K., Miss Archibald.

(DOREEN *exits to the kitchen.*

LOTTA *and* MAUD *enter* R *in the hall and talk to* MISS ARCHIE. BONITA *picks up a plate of sandwiches, takes a sandwich, then passes the plate to* DEIRDRE, *who puts it on the card table.* ALMINA *takes a sandwich from the plate on the coffee-table, retreats to the tub chair and sits*)

CORA (*sitting in the easy chair down* L) I'm absolutely exhausted. I thought that ass with the zither would never stop.

ALMINA. He was certainly very handsome.

CORA. His handsomeness palled on me after the first three-quarters of an hour.

MAUD (*crossing to the coffee-table*) Personally, I'm going straight up to bed. (*She takes some sandwiches*) I'll take a couple of sandwiches with me. (*She moves to the stairs*) I don't want any soup, it might wake me up.

(MAUD *exits up the stairs amid a general murmur of* "good nights". LOTTA *moves and stands above the card table*)

MISS ARCHIE (*crossing to the coffee-table*) How was the rehearsal? (*She picks up the plate of sandwiches and offers it to May*)

(MAY *refuses a sandwich.* MISS ARCHIE *crosses and offers the plate to* ESTELLE *and* CORA *who each take a sandwich*)

Lotta (*taking a sandwich from the plate on the card table*) Very good, but I fear much too long. I suppose they have to have all these microphones. They spoil it for me rather.

Cora. None of them nowadays can project their voice beyond a whisper.

(Doreen *enters from the kitchen carrying a tray with eight bowls of soup which she puts down rather awkwardly on the coffee-table.* Miss Archie *crosses to Almina and offers her a sandwich.* Almina *rises and takes the whole plate*)

Lotta. I thought Marjorie Atherton's dance with all the men was very charming.

Cora. Very, considering that she can't put one foot in front of the other.

(Lotta *moves to the piano.* Miss Archie *and* Almina *stand up* l *of the coffee-table*)

Sarita (*pointing to Doreen*) There's that girl who brings me my breakfast. What's she doing here?

Almina (*in a false, rather cooing voice*) That's Doreen, dear—you remember Doreen, don't you?

Sarita (*graciously*) Of course I do. We shared digs in Wolverhampton years and years ago.

(Almina *takes the plate of sandwiches to the tub chair and sits*)

(*To Bonita*) Do you know, our landlady was an absolute horror, and one night she locked us out and we hammered and hammered on the door and I had to crawl in through the scullery window. (*To Doreen*) Don't you remember?

Doreen (*startled*) Well, Miss Myrtle, I . . .

(Bonita *rises, picks up two bowls of soup, goes to* r *of the card table and gives one to Deirdre*)

Bonita. Of course she remembers. Who would forget a thing like that?

Miss Archie (*moving* c) You can hop off to bed now, Doreen.

Doreen (*running to the hall*) O.K., Miss Archie, thanks.

(Miss Archie *takes two bowls of soup, gives one to Lotta and one to Almina, then returns to the coffee-table*)

Lotta. Thank you for waiting up for us, Doreen, I'm afraid you must be very tired.

Doreen. It's a pleasure, I'm sure, miss.

Sarita. Don't forget to turn the gas out on the landing, we promised Mrs Worsley we would and we don't want any more scenes.

Doreen. O.K., Miss Myrtle.

(DOREEN *exits to the kitchen.* ESTELLE *rises, goes to the coffee-table and picks up two bowls of soup*)

SARITA (*to Bonita*) Head like a sieve, that girl, no concentration. (*She rises and addresses Estelle across the coffee-table*) She dried up dead in the first act last night, just stood there with her mouth —(*she gestures with her fingers and thumb*) opening and shutting silently, like a carp. Poor Ronnie was frantic.

(ESTELLE *crosses to Cora, gives her a bowl of soup, then sits on the fire-stool*)

MISS ARCHIE (*taking Sarita gently by the arm*) Bedtime, now, old dear. (*She leads Sarita to the stairs*)

SARITA (*without protest*) I know. I know—can't afford to lose our beauty sleep. (*To Bonita*) Train call tomorrow at nine-thirty —oh, dear. (*She goes slowly up the stairs*) I must remember to give a little present to that girl who keeps on running about. What *is* her name?

MISS ARCHIE (*following Sarita up the stairs*) "Doreen", dear.

SARITA (*on the landing*) Poor child, fancy being saddled with a name like that. Sounds like an eye lotion.

(SARITA *and* MISS ARCHIE *exit on the landing*)

BONITA. Well, girls, here's to the *Midnight Matinée* from which all our blessings flow. (*She raises her bowl of soup*)

LOTTA. And to all those very kind people who worked so hard for it.

BONITA. Hear, hear!

(*They drink the toast.* BONITA *removes her coat, puts it over the back of a chair, then sits* R *of the card table*)

ESTELLE. Poor old Sarita. Do you think she'll ever get any better, or just go on and on getting madder and madder?

BONITA. She'll probably stay about the same. She's quite happy most of the time; at least, that's what Dr Jevons says.

(LOTTA *moves to the coffee-table and puts down her bowl*)

LOTTA. It's a form of escape, isn't it? (*She looks at May*)

BONITA. Yes, I suppose so.

(ALMINA *puts her plate and bowl on the piano*)

LOTTA. Miss Archie's wonderful with her. (*She picks up a bowl of soup*)

BONITA. Miss Archie's a pretty good sort taken all round.

CORA. If only she didn't make us feel we ought to present arms all the time.

(LOTTA *takes the bowl of soup to May*)

LOTTA. Here's some soup, May.

(*The others all watch while* MAY *turns her head away in silence*)

I said, here's some soup, May. Would you like it or not?

(MAY *still ignores her*)

Are you never going to break down?

DEIRDRE (*rising and crossing to* R *of Lotta*) Ah, for goodness' sake, May Davenport, it's shame you should be feeling, walking through the last years of your life with your head so high and your heart so full of hatred.

MAY. Please don't talk to me like that and mind your own business.

LOTTA. It is Deirdre's business, May. It's the business of all of us in this house to live together as amicably as possible without causing each other any embarrassment.

DEIRDRE. If you'll take my advice you'll pay no attention to her. She's warming her cold heart at the fire of her own hatred. Take that away and she'll freeze to death, you mark my words.

LOTTA (*crossing and replacing the bowl on the coffee-table*) I'll mark them, Deirdre. But I fear at the present moment they are not being very helpful.

DEIRDRE (*crossing to the stairs*) Well, the sweet waters of oblivion for me. (*She goes up the stairs*) I'll say a couple of Hail Marys before I drop off in case the Good Lord should see fit to gather me to His bosom in the middle of the night.

LOTTA. Somehow I don't feel that he will. Good night, Deirdre.

(DEIRDRE *exits on the landing*)

(*Firmly*) May. May, I want to talk to you.

(MAY *rises and without looking at Lotta moves towards the stairs.* LOTTA *intercepts May and holds her wrists. The others, except* CORA, *look away in embarrassment*)

MAY (*icily*) Please let me pass.

LOTTA. I have no intention of letting you pass, nor have I any intention of allowing you to carry on this idiocy any longer. We have now been in this house together for a month without addressing a word to each other and the situation is intolerable. You are going to listen to what I have to say so you had better make up your mind to it. (*She releases May*)

MAY. I am not. (*She makes a movement towards the stairs*)

LOTTA (*gripping May firmly by the arms*) Stay where you are.

MAY. Leave go of me immediately. You must be out of your mind.

LOTTA. Listen to me. I implore you to listen to me. Not for my sake—I don't care if you never speak to me again—but for the sake of all the other people in this house. This age-old feud must be resolved here and now. If we were living our ordinary lives it would be different: we could go on avoiding each other as we have done for the last thirty years, but here we can't. Here, we are forced to see each other, morning, noon and night until we die. We had better face this fact, May. We have fallen on evil days and there is no sense in making them more evil than they need be. Do let us, for God's sake, forget the past and welcome our limited future with as much grace as possible. (*She releases May and steps back*)

MAY. Eloquently put, Lotta. I would be the last to deny your sentimental appeal to an audience. (*She pauses*)

(LOTTA *moves to the piano*)

(*She moves to the foot of the stairs and turns*) It was all you ever had. (*She turns and goes silently up the stairs to the landing*)

BONITA. Once a ham always a ham.

(MAY *glares at Bonita, then exits on the landing*)

LOTTA (*moving c; hopelessly*) I did my best. I shan't try any more. (*She crosses to Estelle*) It's a waste of time and there's so little time left. (*She bites her lip and forces a smile*) Thank God.

CURTAIN

ACT II

SCENE I

SCENE—*The same. A Sunday afternoon in the following September.*

Before the CURTAIN *rises, the music of "Waiting in the Wings" is heard.*

When the CURTAIN *rises, the room is empty. The fire is lit and the french windows are closed. The music fades. The sound of the front-door bell is heard.* DOREEN *enters from the kitchen and exits* R *in the hall. The front door slams.*

DOREEN (*off*) Hullo, sir.
PERRY (*off*) Hullo, Doreen. How are you?
DOREEN (*off*) Smashing, thanks.
ZELDA (*off*) Through here, is it?

(ZELDA FENWICK *enters from the hall and moves* C. PERRY *and* DOREEN *follow her on.* ZELDA *is in her middle thirties. She is nice-looking, trim, and wears well-cut trousers and a sports shirt. She looks around the room with interest*)

PERRY (*moving above the card table*) Where is everyone, Doreen?
DOREEN (*moving to* L *of Perry*) Upstairs, I think, all except Miss Clarke and Miss Davenport—they've gone for a walk.
PERRY. Is Miss Archie in her office?
DOREEN. Yes, sir.
PERRY. You might tell her we're here.
DOREEN. O.K., sir.

(DOREEN *looks at* Zelda, *runs across to the door* L, *knocks on it and exits*)

ZELDA. Quite a nice room. (*She indicates the bust*) Who's that?
PERRY. Sir Hilary Brooks. He founded the place.
ZELDA. My mother was crazy about him when she was young; used to wait in pit queues for hours and hours. I have a feeling he was rather an old ham. (*She looks up at the portrait over the fireplace*) My grandmother was crazy about her.
PERRY (*moving behind the sofa*) A keen theatre-going family.
ZELDA. Good Lord, yes. They never stopped. I was dragged screaming to matinées from the age of four onwards.
PERRY. Didn't you enjoy them?
ZELDA (*sitting in the armchair* LC) Not the jolly pantomimes and children's plays. I can't think of *Peter Pan* to this day without a shudder.
PERRY. I love *Peter Pan*.

30

Zelda. That's because you've got a mother fixation. All sensitive lads with mother fixations worship *Peter Pan*.

Perry. I expect I have a crocodile fixation, too.

(Doreen *enters* l *and crosses to* c)

Doreen. Miss Archibald says she won't be a minute.

Perry. Thanks, Doreen.

(Doreen *looks at Zelda again, then at Perry, grins and exits to the kitchen.* Zelda *takes out a packet of cigarettes and offers them to Perry*)

Zelda. Cigarette?

Perry. No, thanks. (*He crosses to* r *of Zelda and lights her cigarette*)

Zelda. Who is the oldest inmate here?

Perry. Martha Carrington. She's pushing ninety-five.

Zelda. Good Lord!

Perry. And what's more, she still has a beau, Osgood Meeker. He's just a kiddie of seventy. He comes to visit her every Sunday—rain or shine. He's probably up with her now. He always brings her violets.

(Zelda *whips out a notebook and scribbles in it*)

Zelda. Good. That's the sort of stuff I want.

Perry (*apprehensively*) You will be careful, won't you? I mean —don't mention names more than you can help.

Zelda. Don't worry, I'll be discretion itself. It's just possible, though, that one or two of them may recognize me.

Perry. I shouldn't think so. You haven't started your new television programme yet.

Zelda. No, but they'll know my name from the column. (*She puts her notebook away*)

Perry. I'll introduce you as Miss—Miss Starkey.

Zelda. Why "Starkey" for Heaven's sake?

Perry. *Peter Pan* again; it's an obsession with me.

Zelda. Where are they going to put the what-you-may-call-it if they get it?

Perry. "Solarium". (*He points to the terrace*) There.

(Zelda *rises and looks towards the terrace*)

We want to glass the whole terrace in. It would mean an awful lot to them to be able to enjoy the sun without the wind. (*He goes to the french windows and opens them*) As it is, they can hardly ever use the terrace unless the weather's absolutely perfect. (*He goes on to the terrace*)

Zelda (*following Perry on to the terrace*) Yes. I see what you mean. The damned house was built in the wrong place to start with.

(Miss Archie *enters* l)

MISS ARCHIE. Hullo, Perry—I didn't hear the old bike.

PERRY (*coming into the room*) No. I came down with a friend.

(ZELDA *comes into the room*)

May I introduce Miss Starkey—Miss Archibald.

ZELDA. How do you do?

MISS ARCHIE (*wringing Zelda's hand*) How do you do?

PERRY. She drives like a fiend. I think she has a Stirling Moss fixation.

MISS ARCHIE (*laughing heartily*) Good show!

ZELDA. I've got an old Jag convertible, quite a nice little job.

MISS ARCHIE. I should just say so. What can you do in her?

ZELDA. Up to a hundred and twenty on the open road.

MISS ARCHIE. Wizard!

PERRY (*moving to the foot of the stairs*) Perhaps I'd better leave you girls to your feminine secrets while I go and put on a pipe or something.

MISS ARCHIE (*ignoring Perry and moving to the fireplace*) I had an M.G. just after the war but I ran it into a lorry.

PERRY. Butter fingers!

ZELDA (*moving* C) Were you Waafs, Wrens or Ats?

MISS ARCHIE. Ensa. (*She puts some coal on the fire*)

ZELDA (*sitting in the armchair* LC) Lord! That must have been a bit tricky, having to deal with all those actors.

MISS ARCHIE (*slightly defensive on behalf of her old regiment*) It was damned interesting. My job of course was mainly administrative, but I managed to get about a bit: Cairo, Bombay, Burma . . . Better than staying at home and pen-pushing in some Ministry.

ZELDA. I was a Wren. Malta for two years.

MISS ARCHIE. Good for you!

PERRY. And now to rescue Wendy! (*He strikes a melodramatic attitude*)

(CORA *and* MAY *enter by the french windows. They are both dressed for walking.* CORA, *seeing Perry, looks surprised*)

CORA. Hullo, Perry. (*She crosses to* C)

(ZELDA *rises*)

PERRY (*moving behind the sofa*) Hullo, Cora. May I introduce an old friend of mine—Miss Starkey—Miss Cora Clarke.

CORA (*shaking hands with Zelda*) How do you do? (*She moves down* RC)

ZELDA. How do you do?

PERRY. And Miss May Davenport.

(MAY *moves to* R *of Zelda*)

ZELDA. How do you do?

MAY (*shaking hands with Zelda*) How do you do?

ZELDA. My father was one of your greatest admirers, Miss Davenport.

MAY. I fear you must be confusing your father with your grandfather, my dear.

PERRY (*hurriedly*) Have you had a nice walk?

MAY. Very pleasant. We managed to hobble to the tow-path and back. (*She looks at Zelda's trousers*) Have you been riding?

ZELDA. Riding? Oh, no, we've just driven down from London.

MAY (*smiling remotely*) How foolish of me.

PERRY. Miss Starkey was most anxious to come and see "The Wings" and everything, so I brought her down to tea.

CORA. How nice. (*To Zelda*) If you'll forgive us for the moment we'll go upstairs and take off our things.

(CORA *exits up the stairs*)

MAY. *A bientôt*, Miss Starkey.

(MAY *exits up the stairs.* ZELDA *watches her intently*)

MISS ARCHIE (*to Zelda*) Cigarette?

ZELDA. No, thanks, I've got one.

PERRY. Is Osgood here today?

MISS ARCHIE. Of course. He never misses a Sunday.

ZELDA (*looking to see that May is out of earshot*) Lotta Bainbridge is here, isn't she?

MISS ARCHIE. Yes. She came in June.

ZELDA (*moving above the sofa; thoughtfully*) Lotta Bainbridge and May Davenport. Wasn't there a famous quarrel or something? I seem to remember hearing about it.

MISS ARCHIE. Yes, there was.

ZELDA. What was it about?

MISS ARCHIE (*guardedly*) I don't know—it was ages ago, anyhow.

ZELDA (*sitting on the upstage arm of the sofa*) Have they kissed and made friends?

(PERRY *moves to* R *of the card table*)

MISS ARCHIE (*uncomfortably*) Well, no—not exactly. Actually it's a bit tricky.

ZELDA. There's a good story in that, isn't there?

MISS ARCHIE (*puzzled*) Story—how do you mean?

ZELDA. "Old foes still feuding in the twilight of their lives."

MISS ARCHIE. Sounds like newspaper stuff.

PERRY (*nervously*) Yes—it does rather—doesn't it?

(OSGOOD *enters down the stairs*)

OSGOOD. Ah, there you are, Miss Archie. (*He crosses to* C)

(MISS ARCHIE *moves to* L *of Osgood*)

I didn't see you when I arrived. (*He shakes hands with Miss Archie*) I went straight up as usual—I hope you don't mind.

MISS ARCHIE. Of course not.

OSGOOD. She's in splendid form today, positively blooming.

MISS ARCHIE. May I?—this is Miss Starkey—Mr Meeker.

ZELDA (*rising*) How do you do?

OSGOOD (*shaking hands with Zelda*) How do you do? (*He salutes Perry*)

(PERRY *bows, then sits* R *of the card table.* MISS ARCHIE *moves to the fire-stool and sits*)

ZELDA. I understand that you visit Miss Carrington every Sunday.

OSGOOD. Oh, yes—yes, ever since she first arrived here, years ago. It has become quite a little ritual, hasn't it, Miss Archie?

MISS ARCHIE. Rather.

OSGOOD. I think—I hope that it gives her pleasure; it seems to.

MISS ARCHIE. Of course it does, Mr Meeker. She looks forward to it all through the week.

ZELDA. How long is it since she retired?

OSGOOD. Oh, many many years, thirty or more. I last saw her in the twenties in *The Late Mrs Robart* at the *St James's*. She was getting on in years even then, but she was as witty and stylish as ever. She had a special way of moving about the stage that was all her own, effortless, and with such infinite grace. I saw her for the first time in nineteen hundred and six in *The Lavender Girl*.

ZELDA. *The Lavender Girl.* That's certainly going back a bit.

OSGOOD. I was only eighteen at the time and I quite lost my heart. Those were her great years, of course, her musical comedy years. There was nobody like her and there never will be again. All London was at her feet.

ZELDA. I remember my parents talking about her. (*She pauses*)

(OSGOOD *chuckles in agreement*)

She hadn't much of a voice, had she?

(OSGOOD *stops short and looks angrily at Zelda*)

OSGOOD. I suppose she hadn't much of anything really, except magic, but she had a great deal of that.

ZELDA. And now she's dying upstairs?

OSGOOD. No, Miss Starkey—living upstairs. I don't think she will ever die, not quite.

ZELDA. Bully for you, Mr Meeker.

OSGOOD. I'm afraid I don't quite understand . . .

MISS ARCHIE (*rising and interrupting to save the situation*) Would you like to have your tea in my office as usual, Mr Meeker, or will you wait and have it with all of us in the dining-room?

OSGOOD. Neither today, thank you, Miss Archie. I have an

appointment in London. I can just catch the four-forty if I hurry.
(*He crosses up* R)

Miss Archie. You're quite sure? It's no trouble.

(Perry *rises*)

Osgood (*stopping and turning*) Quite sure. Thank you all the
same. You're always so kind. Good-bye, Mr Lascoe.

Perry. Good-bye, sir—until next Sunday.

Osgood. Oh, yes—yes—next Sunday. Good-bye, Miss Starkey.

Zelda. Good-bye.

Osgood. Your parents were quite right, she hadn't much of a
voice, but it didn't matter—I really do assure you it didn't
matter in the least.

(Osgood *exits* R *in the hall*)

Zelda (*moving up* C) There's certainly gold in these yar hills.
(*To Miss Archie*) Would it be all right if I took a few shots of the
house from the garden?

(Perry *coughs warningly*)

The light's still good.

Miss Archie (*more and more puzzled*) Shots?

Zelda. Snapshots. For my memory book. My camera's in the
car.

Perry (*moving towards Zelda*) I'll get it.

Zelda. No—don't you trouble. I'd like to wander round on
my own for a bit, anyhow. I shan't be long.

(Zelda *exits on the terrace*)

Miss Archie. What *is* going on?

Perry (*moving above the sofa*) How do you mean?

Miss Archie. Who is she, Perry?

Perry (*moving down* R *of the sofa*) I told you. She's an old
friend of mine—Miss Starkey.

Miss Archie. You're up to something.

Perry (*moving below the sofa*) Don't be silly. What would I be
up to?

Miss Archie. She's Press, isn't she?

(*There is a pause.* Perry *sits on the sofa at the downstage end*)

Perry. Yes—she's Zelda Fenwick.

Miss Archie. Zelda Fenwick! The one that writes all that hog-
wash in the *Clarion?*

Perry (*unhappily*) Yes.

Miss Archie (*moving* C) Good God, have you gone out of your
mind? You know Press interviews are dead against the rules.

Perry. She has a lot of influence.

Miss Archie. Do any of the committee know she's here?

PERRY. Of course not. It was my idea.

MISS ARCHIE. Look here, my lad, you're going to get yourself into serious trouble.

PERRY. I don't care. I want the old girls to get that Solarium. The committee has dug its feet in, I've done everything I can to persuade them but they're as stubborn as mules. The Fund could afford it perfectly well. I've got another estimate, from Weatherby's; only eighteen hundred.

MISS ARCHIE (*moving to the fireplace*) What has all this got to do with Zelda Fenwick?

PERRY. I said that if she'd promise to make an appeal for us on her television programme, I'd arrange for her to have an exclusive story on "The Wings".

MISS ARCHIE. You'll get the sack. You'll get us both the sack. (*She moves to the french windows*) Why the hell didn't you consult me first?

PERRY. You needn't know anything about it. I'll take the rap.

MISS ARCHIE. I can't agree to it. You'll have to get her out, and quick—pack up the whole idea.

PERRY (*rising and crossing to Miss Archie*) Don't get into such a frizz. She's promised to let me see whatever she writes before it goes in.

MISS ARCHIE. I've heard that one before. (*She moves to the fireplace*) I don't like it, Perry—I don't like it one little bit. It's going dead against regulations.

PERRY. The old girls have built up this Solarium in their minds as the one thing in the world they really want. I don't see why they should be deprived of it just because some dizzy fathead like Boodie Nethersole talks a lot of hot air about "needless expenditure".

MISS ARCHIE. Who were in favour of it?

PERRY. Laura, Dame Maggie, old Cecil Murdock. A few of the others were wavering but they allowed themselves to be over-ruled.

MISS ARCHIE (*striding up* C) Damn it—I don't know what to think.

PERRY. It isn't needless expenditure, anyway. It would make a very real difference to their health and comfort.

MISS ARCHIE (*after a pause*) All right, I'll play ball.

PERRY (*moving to Miss Archie and hugging her*) Atta, girl!

MISS ARCHIE. We shall probably find ourselves up the old creek but they can't fire us both.

PERRY. They can but they won't. They'd have to find replacements, and the few of them that really take an interest and do the work, like Laura and Dame Maggie, know damn well that's easier said than done.

MISS ARCHIE (*glancing towards the french windows*) Look out, someone's coming. (*She crosses to the door* L) Let's go into my office.

(MISS ARCHIE *and* PERRY *exit hurriedly* L.

ZELDA *enters on the terrace, carrying a camera. She focuses the camera off* R *and takes a picture.*

SARITA *enters on the landing and comes cautiously down the stairs, singing to herself. She is, as usual, in dressing-gown and slippers. She crosses to* C, *looks at the fireplace, sees some matches on the mantelpiece, claps her hands, hurries to the fireplace and picks up the matches.* ZELDA, *on the terrace, watches.* SARITA *sits in the armchair* LC *with a little giggle.* ZELDA *comes into the room, puts the camera on the piano and moves to* R *of Sarita*)

ZELDA. Hullo.

SARITA (*holding out her hand; grandly*) How do you do?

ZELDA (*shaking hands with Sarita*) How do you do?

SARITA. I'm afraid my sister is at a rehearsal, but she is sure to be back soon. Won't you sit down?

ZELDA (*sitting on the sofa*) Thank you.

SARITA (*striking a match*) Isn't that pretty?

ZELDA (*slightly bewildered*) Yes. Very pretty.

SARITA. When we were very young we used to have boxes of coloured matches on Guy Fawkes Day and the tips of them were different from ordinary matches, longer and fatter, like little black sausages. (*She throws the match gracefully into the fire*) When you struck them they were like red and green stars.

ZELDA. You must forgive my ignorance, but I don't know your name. Mine is Zelda F—Starkey.

SARITA. Miserable Starkey!

ZELDA (*ignoring this*) What's yours?

SARITA. I am Sarita Myrtle. I expect that surprises you, doesn't it?

ZELDA (*at sea*) Oh, yes—oh, yes, of course.

SARITA. I've always looked so much younger than my age. It's an advantage in a way, of course, but one can't go on playing *ingénues* for ever, can one?

ZELDA. How long have you been here?

SARITA. Oh, quite a while.

ZELDA. It's a very nice house, isn't it?

SARITA. Capacity.

ZELDA (*pressing on*) Are you happy here, on the whole?

SARITA. Oh, yes, except on matinée days—I hate those tea trays, so distracting.

ZELDA. Are they kind to you?

SARITA. Oh, yes. Sometimes they're a little dull in the first act, but they generally warm up.

ZELDA. Is your room comfortable?

SARITA. It's cold. (*She rises, moves to* L *of Zelda and indicates the door* L) *She* says it isn't because it's next to the airing cupboard, but she doesn't always speak the truth, I'm afraid.

B*

ZELDA. Is "she" Miss Archibald?
SARITA. Yes, I think so.

(DEIRDRE *enters from the television room and stands watching Sarita*)

It's difficult to be quite sure, people's faces change so, it's very confusing. (*She strikes another match*) There!

(ESTELLE *enters from the television room*)

DEIRDRE (*crossing quickly to Sarita*) What the hell are you doing with those matches, Sarita Myrtle? Is it burning us all to cinders that you're after? (*She takes the box from Sarita and puts it on the piano*) Go back to your bed this very minute.

(SARITA *throws the match away, moves to Deirdre and holds out her hand*)

SARITA (*sociably*) How do you do?
DEIRDRE. Never you mind how I do. (*She takes Sarita's arm and leads her to the stairs*) Come away with you before Miss Archie catches you and claps you in irons. Take her arm, Estelle.
SARITA (*shaking herself free*) For Heaven's sake, keep your voice down, Rupert. The children will hear.
ESTELLE (*taking Sarita's arm*) Come, dear . . .
SARITA (*throwing Estelle's hand off; grandly*) Henceforward, Mr Cartwright, we must regard one another as strangers. (*She goes up the stairs and poses at the top*) I can say no more—farewell.

(SARITA *exits on the landing.* ZELDA *rises and crosses to the fireplace*)

DEIRDRE. Go after her, Estelle, and see her safe in her bed. You have more of a way with her than I have.
ESTELLE (*resigned*) Very well. I hope this isn't the beginning of one of her bad spells. (*To* ZELDA) Excuse me.

(ESTELLE *exits up the stairs*)

DEIRDRE (*crossing to* ZELDA) The poor ould thing's a bit weak in the head.
ZELDA. Yes, I gathered that.
DEIRDRE. My name is Deirdre O'Malley. Are you a friend of Miss Archie's?
ZELDA. No. As a matter of fact I came down with Perry Lascoe. I'm just a stray visitor. I've heard so much about "The Wings" and I wanted to see it for myself. My name is Starkey.
DEIRDRE (*shaking hands with* ZELDA) It's a pleasure to meet you, I'm sure. A new face is always a bit of a treat—we get tired of looking at our own ould ones year in year out. (*She crosses to the sofa*)
ZELDA. Have you been here long?

DEIRDRE. Nearly twenty years. (*She sits on the sofa at the upstage end*) I've seen a lot of them come and go but the Good Lord has seen fit to let me linger on.

ZELDA (*moving c*) Are you happy here?

DEIRDRE. As happy as you could expect a bunch of old women to be when the tide of life has turned away from them and they are left high and dry waiting for the grave.

ZELDA. Is the food good?

DEIRDRE. That's a practical question and deserves a practical answer. No, it is not.

ZELDA. What's wrong with it?

DEIRDRE. You're not one of the committee, are you?

ZELDA. No.

DEIRDRE. Good. I'd have a few home truths to tell you if you were.

ZELDA. Don't you approve of the committee?

DEIRDRE. Approve of them! (*She gives a short laugh*) They don't give us a chance to approve of them. We don't clap eyes on them from one year's end to the other. Just one or two of them have the grace to come down here once in a blue moon. They're given tea and then they drive away in all their finery and we're left feeling like a lot of animals in the Zoo. I'm sometimes surprised that they don't prod us with their umbrellas and throw us buns.

ZELDA. Aren't you being a little bitter, Miss O'Malley?

DEIRDRE. Bitter, is it? You'd be bitter if the last years of your life were controlled by a lot of gabbing flipperty-gibbets who don't really give a hoot in hell whether you're alive or dead.

(BONITA *and* MAUD *enter down the stairs*)

MAUD (*as she enters*) If I got a notice like that I'd never lift my head up again.

BONITA. The *Sunday Times* was very good.

MAUD. Yes, but I couldn't understand half of it; too many French words and that Edwigger what's-her-name being dragged in all the time.

BONITA. Not "Edwigger", dear—"Edveege". Edveege Fooyare. (*She sees Zelda and crosses to R of her*) Oh—how do you do?

DEIRDRE. This is a friend of Perry's—Miss—Miss . . .

ZELDA. Starkey.

BONITA. I'm Bonita Belgrave. (*She shakes hands with Zelda, then crosses to L of her*) And this is Maud Melrose.

MAUD (*moving to R of Zelda and shaking hands with her*) How do you do? Where *is* Perry?

ZELDA. I don't know. He seems to have disappeared.

(MAUD *goes up* R *and looks into the hall.*
   MAY *and* ESTELLE *enter on the landing.* MAY *carries her embroidery bag*)

ESTELLE (*as she enters*) Boodie Nethersole got wonderful notices in that play at the *Arts*. (*She comes down the stairs*)

(MAY *follows Estelle down the stairs*)

The *Sunday Times* says that the only actress in the world who could have played it better would have been Edveege Fooyare.

(MAUD *and* BONITA *join in the last two words under their breath*)

MAY. I'm beginning to think that the *Sunday Times* must be subsidized by the French Government.

(MAUD *sits* R *of the card table.*
ALMINA *and* CORA *enter down the stairs.*
PERRY *and* MISS ARCHIE *enter* L)

BONITA. Why, Perry, I thought you'd deserted us.
PERRY. No, Miss Archie and I have been having a little gossip.
BONITA (*to* Zelda) Is that your car outside?
ZELDA. Yes.
BONITA. It's a beauty, isn't it? I saw it from the lavatory window.
MAY. Really, my dear Bonita! There is no need to be over-explicit.

(ALMINA *crosses to* PERRY *who introduces her to* Zelda. CORA *moves behind the sofa.* PERRY *settles* ALMINA *in the tub chair*)

BONITA. Well, I couldn't have seen it from my own window because it faces in the opposite direction. (*She crosses to the easy chair down* L *and sits*)

(MAY *crosses to the armchair* LC, *sits and takes out her embroidery.* ESTELLE *sits in the armchair up* L)

DEIRDRE (*mournfully*) When I think of the changes in the world during the span of my own miserable lifetime me head reels, and that's no lie.

(ZELDA *crosses to the fireplace*)

CORA. Your life span hasn't been in the least miserable, Deirdre. You've enjoyed every minute of it and still do.
DEIRDRE. And what is there to enjoy I should like to know? Loitering about here in me dotage, getting feebler and wearier with every blessed breath I take.
CORA. Pay no attention to Deirdre, Miss Starkey. She loves talking like that.
MAY. She also takes considerable pleasure in embarrassing the rest of us.
DEIRDRE. Maybe it's the unacceptable ring of truth behind me words that embarrasses you, May Davenport.

MAY. I wish you would either address me as "May" or "Miss Davenport", Deirdre. "May Davenport" sounds like a roll call.

DEIRDRE. You can save your almighty arrogance until you get to the final roll call, Miss May Davenport.

MISS ARCHIE (*firmly*) Now then, Deirdre. That's no way to talk when there are strangers present.

DEIRDRE. Nothing I do is right, nothing I say is right. If I fell into the dark waters of the river this very night, I doubt if anyone would lift a finger to help me.

MAY. The Irish can never resist cheap sentimentality.

(LOTTA *enters down the stairs*)

BONITA. Oh, May, don't make things worse, for Heaven's sake.

LOTTA (*moving up R of the sofa*) What on earth's happening?

BONITA. Nothing much. Deirdre's getting a bit out of hand, that's all.

DEIRDRE. Out of hand, is it . . .

BONITA. Yes, it is. Be quiet.

PERRY. Lotta. I don't think you've met Miss Starkey.

ZELDA (*moving* C) Hallo, how are you?

LOTTA (*crossing to Zelda and shaking hands*) Miss Starkey? (*She stares at Zelda*)

ZELDA. Yes. I came down with Perry. We're old friends.

LOTTA. Is Starkey your private name?

ZELDA. Private name? I . . .

LOTTA. You're really Zelda Fenwick, aren't you—the one who writes the "People are News" column in the *Sunday Clarion*?

ZELDA (*after a slight pause*) Yes. Yes, I am.

(*There is general reaction*)

MISS ARCHIE. Oh, Lord—that's torn it.

MAY (*rising*) Is this true, Perry?

PERRY (*guiltily*) Yes. Perfectly true.

LOTTA (*to Zelda*) I saw you on television a few weeks ago. (*She turns to Perry*) I think, Perry, that it would have been more polite and considerate if you had introduced Miss Fenwick by her proper name.

PERRY (*miserably*) I'll explain it later. I'll explain it all later.

LOTTA. I'm sure that no explanation is in the least necessary. (*She crosses to the sofa and sits*) It's merely a little confusing, that's all.

MAY. I beg to differ. A great deal of explanation is necessary. (*To Zelda*) May I ask, Miss Fenwick, if you are here in a professional capacity?

ZELDA (*with spirit*) I am always in a professional capacity, Miss Davenport. That is an essential part of my job.

MAY (*moving down* LC) Is the committee aware of your visit to us?

ZELDA. No. And if I may say so, I rather resent your tone. I am not answerable to you for my actions or to your committee.

(*There is general reaction.* ESTELLE *rises and goes to Almina*)

PERRY (*moving* C) Just a minute—please let me explain.
MAY (*in rich tones*) Be quiet, Perry.
LOTTA (*with considerable authority*) It seems to me that the situation is being rather over-dramatized.

(MAY *starts to interrupt*)

No, May. I'm afraid I must insist on speaking.

(PERRY *and* MISS ARCHIE *take refuge up* C *by the piano.* MAY *crosses to* BONITA *who holds her hand*)

I am sure Miss Fenwick will be the first to realize that it will place us all in a most humiliating position if she mentions either "The Wings" itself or any of its occupants in her newspaper. In the first place it would be a breach of the rules of this—(*she smiles*) this rather "specialized" charity, and in the second place I am sure that, even in her professional capacity, she would not wish either to betray our confidence or abuse our hospitality. I am right, aren't I, Miss Fenwick?
ZELDA (*awkwardly*) Well—er—as a matter of fact . . .
LOTTA (*rising*) You will promise, won't you, even if you had it in mind to write a story about us, *not* to write it? We are happy enough here, living out our days in this most agreeable backwater. The last thing any of us wants is publicity. It would shed too harsh a light on us, show up all our lines and wrinkles. That would be an unkind thing to do, wouldn't it? We are still actresses in our hearts. We'd like to be remembered as we were, not as we are. You will give us your promise, won't you?
ZELDA. I appreciate what you say, Miss Bainbridge. But I'm afraid I must be honest with you. My editor has been trying to get a story on this place for years.

(*There is general reaction*)

(*To all of them*) I know you will understand that it isn't only in the theatre that the job must come first. I cannot promise not to write about "The Wings"——

(*There is general reaction*)

MAY. Well, I would like to say . . .
ZELDA. —but I can promise to do all I can to help. I have already arranged with Perry that if he let me come here that I would make an appeal on my T.V. programme for your Solarium.
CORA. Solarium—Good God—are we to sell our souls to get that damned Solarium? (*She moves down* RC)
LOTTA. Oh, Cora—please. (*She sits on the sofa*)

MAY (*moving to the upstage end of the fireplace*) I'm ashamed of you, Perry. Mortally, mortally ashamed.

MISS ARCHIE (*moving* C) Here, steady on. It's no good flying off the handle at Perry. He only did it for the best.

ESTELLE (*moving to May; wailing*) It's all my fault—I was the one who suggested it in the first place.

(MAY *comforts* ESTELLE)

DEIRDRE (*rising dramatically*) Shame on you, Miss whatever-your-name-is. Shame on you, I say! And may God forgive you for making a mock of a houseful of poor defenceless old women who are only asking to be left in peace and quiet. The devil's curse on you for being a double-face, scheming hypocrite. Write what you like and be damned to you. I've said my say. (*She sits on the sofa*)

LOTTA. You certainly have, Deirdre. And I for one would like to throttle you.

ZELDA (*moving to the piano and collecting her camera*) I can't stand any more of this. Are you coming, Perry?

PERRY (*wretchedly*) No. I've got to stay here.

ZELDA (*curtly*) Good-bye, everybody. I'm sorry to have caused such a hullabaloo.

(ZELDA *exits* R *in the hall.* PERRY *and* MISS ARCHIE *move towards the hall. The front door is heard to slam.* PERRY *and* MISS ARCHIE *stop.* MAY *moves* LC)

MAY (*in stentorian tones*) The whole thing is an outrage—an outrage!

(MAUD *tidies the cards on the card table*)

CORA (*moving behind the sofa*) For Heaven's sake calm down, May.

MAY. The committee must be warned immediately, pressure must be brought to bear.

BONITA (*rising and moving down* R) Personally, I think a great deal of fuss is being made about nothing.

(MAUD *rises*)

What does it really matter whether she writes about us or not?

MAY. We shall be publicly degraded.

CORA. Nonsense!

LOTTA. She'll probably write a lot of sentimental rubbish which will embarrass us for a little until we forget it and everyone else does, too.

CORA. Let's go in to tea and talk about something else. (*She moves up* R)

(BONITA *and* MAUD *exit* R *in the hall.* ESTELLE *goes to* ALMINA, *helps her to rise and exits with her R in the hall. They all talk angrily as they go)*

PERRY. May, I really am sorry.
MAY. Don't speak to me.

(MAY *crosses and exits R in the hall with* CORA. DEIRDRE *rises and moves up R.* LOTTA *rises)*

PERRY (*moving to Lotta*) Lotta, I did it for the best, honestly I did.
LOTTA. I'm sure you did, Perry, but if you will forgive my saying so, it was an error in taste.

(LOTTA *exits R in the hall with* DEIRDRE. MISS ARCHIE *moves towards the hall and turns)*

MISS ARCHIE. Come on, old chap.
PERRY. I don't want any tea.
MISS ARCHIE (*moving above the sofa*) Cheer up! It'll all blow over.
PERRY (*crossing to L*) An error in taste. I suppose it was, really —but I didn't see it like that.
MISS ARCHIE. I don't feel like tea, either. (*She crosses to L*) Let's pop into my office and have a slug of something a bit stronger.

MISS ARCHIE *and* PERRY *exit L. The stage is empty for a moment.*
SARITA *enters on the landing and comes quietly down the stairs. She makes a bee-line for the matches on the piano, strikes one and delightedly watches it burn, then hearing someone coming she hides L of the sofa.*
DOREEN *enters from the kitchen carrying a tray of tea-things. She exits with it R in the hall.*
SARITA *rises, collects another box of matches from the coffee-table and, clutching both boxes, exits quietly up the stairs as—*

the CURTAIN *falls*

SCENE 2

SCENE—*The same. Several hours later.*

Before the CURTAIN *rises, the music of "Miss Mouse" is heard.*

When the CURTAIN *rises, the stage is empty and in darkness except for the glow of the fire. It is the early hours of the morning. Smoke is coming from the landing exit. The music fades and there is silence for a few moments, suddenly broken by a pandemonium of voices from upstairs.* BONITA, *in a dressing-gown, enters on the landing.*

BONITA (*as she enters; calling over her shoulder*) It's coming from Sarita's room. Wake the others, Deirdre. I'll fetch Miss Archie.

(*She comes swiftly down the stairs, crosses to the door* L, *bangs on it and calls*) Miss Archie!

    (*A light appears behind the door* L.
    MAY *enters on the landing and switches on the wall-bracket*)

Miss Archie—come quickly.

    (MISS ARCHIE, *in pyjamas, enters* L)

MISS ARCHIE. What is it?
BONITA. Sarita's room is on fire.
MISS ARCHIE. Sarita's room on fire?

    (MAY *comes down the stairs*)

(*She crosses and goes up the stairs*) No panic, now. Keep calm, every-body. Out of the way, Miss Davenport—I must get to the fire extinguisher.

    (MISS ARCHIE *grabs the fire extinguisher from the wall and exits on the landing*)

(*Off*) All form up in your regular lines and wait for orders.
MAY (*moving down* RC) Has anyone telephoned the fire brigade?
BONITA (*moving down* LC) No—not yet.
MAY. Then I suggest we do so immediately. Come and help me find the number. I've left my glasses upstairs.
BONITA. So have I.

    (MAUD *enters down the stairs and goes to the french windows*)

MAY. In that case we will dial nine-nine-nine. Nine comes one before the O. We can't miss it.

    (MAY *and* BONITA *cross and exit* L. MAUD *opens the french windows*)

MISS ARCHIE (*off*) Bang the nozzle against the wall. There.

    (CORA *enters down the stairs and crosses to* L)

CORA. For God's sake, somebody, shut that window. Having escaped death by burning, it would be idiotic to die of pneu-monia. (*She switches on the wall-brackets* L)

    (ESTELLE *and* ALMINA *enter down the stairs.* ESTELLE *sits in the tub chair.* ALMINA *sits below the card table*)

MAUD (*closing the windows*) I only opened it to let the smoke out—we were suffocating.
ESTELLE. Poor Sarita, poor Sarita.

    (MISS ARCHIE *enters on the landing*)

MISS ARCHIE. It's all right—everything's under control. It was only the curtains that caught fire and I've got them out.

(Miss Archie *exits on the landing.*

Lotta *and* Sarita *enter down the stairs.* Sarita *is wrapped in a blanket. She sits in the armchair* lc.

Bonita *enters* l)

Bonita. Has anyone got any glasses? We can't see the damned dial. We've tried nine-nine-nine but nothing's happened.

Maud. It doesn't matter. It was only the curtains and Miss Archie's put them out.

Bonita. Thank God.

(Bonita *exits* l. Cora *stands behind the armchair* lc.

Deirdre *enters down the stairs*)

Sarita. It looked so pretty—so very pretty.

Deirdre (*on the stairs*) Pretty indeed! It's small thanks to you, Sarita Myrtle, that we're not all charred corpses at this very minute——

(Lotta *gets the fire-stool, places it* l *of Sarita and sits.* Cora *crosses to the upstage end of the sofa*)

—burnt to bloody crisps in our beds. We should have been if I hadn't smelt the smoke.

Sarita (*picking at her blanket*) Why am I wearing this strange garment? Is it to be an oriental production?

(May *and* Bonita *enter* l *and cross to* lc. Deirdre *moves and sits on the sofa at the downstage end*)

May. How did she get hold of the matches?

Bonita. She must have pinched them when nobody was looking and hidden them somewhere. You know Miss Archie always searches her room thoroughly every night.

Deirdre. It's as much as our lives are worth to have her in the house a minute longer.

(Bonita *crosses and stands behind the sofa*)

May. Calm down, Deirdre.

Deirdre. I'll calm down when I feel like it, and not before, and you can put that in your high and mighty pipe and smoke it, May Davenport.

(May *goes to the fire and pokes it*)

Bonita. I'm going to wake Doreen. (*She moves up* c *and switches on the wall-bracket* r) Miss Archie can't cope with everything by herself.

(Bonita *exits to the kitchen*)

Maud. Do you think we ought to telephone to Dr Jevons?

Cora (*sitting on the upstage arm of the sofa*) What for?

Maud. For Sarita, of course. He might give her a sedative or something.

Deirdre. Tell him to bring a strait-jacket while he's at it.

Lotta. Do be quiet, Deirdre. It's unkind to say things like that. (*She pauses*) Oh, dear—I wonder how poor old Martha is —I'd better go and see.

Maud (*crossing to the stairs*) I'll go, Lotta—stay where you are. I've got to get some cigarettes, anyhow. I'm shaking like a leaf.

(Maud *exits up the stairs. The smoke has by now subsided.*
Bonita *and* Doreen *enter from the kitchen.* Doreen *is attired in a pink Japanese kimono and her hair is in kirby grips*)

Bonita (*giving Doreen a slight push*) Run along up and help Miss Archie.

Doreen. Okay, Miss Belgrave. (*She goes up the stairs*) Ooh! What a terrible smell of burning.

(Doreen *exits on the landing.* Bonita *stands behind the sofa*)

Deirdre. What do you expect, with the whole house blazing to the skies? That one's a half-wit.

Lotta. The house isn't blazing to the skies, Deirdre.

Deirdre. It might well be if I hadn't noticed that smoke curling under me door like a grey serpent.

Bonita. I know what I could do with and that's a nip of whisky. I've got some in my room. How about you, Cora?

Cora. Thanks.

Bonita. Any other offers? Lotta—May?

(*All except* May *assent with enthusiasm*)

May. No, thank you, my dear Bonita. (*She sits in the easy chair down* l)

Lotta (*rising*) I should love a little. You're very kind.

Bonita (*moving to the stairs*) I'll fetch the bottle.

(Bonita *exits up the stairs*)

Lotta (*crossing to Cora*) Stay by Sarita, Cora, while I go and find some glasses.

(Lotta *exits to the kitchen*)

Sarita. What are we all waiting here for in the middle of the night? Is someone going to read a play to us?

Deirdre. I'd throttle anybody who tried.

(Maud *enters down the stairs, carrying a packet of cigarettes and a lighter*)

Maud (*moving to* l *of Cora*) Martha's all right.

(Cora *rises*)

She's fast asleep, but poor Miss Archie's wet through. Cigarette, anybody?

CORA *(taking a cigarette)* Thanks, I'd love one.

(LOTTA *enters from the kitchen with a tray of glasses and a jug of water which she puts on the card table*)

ESTELLE *(rising)* Oh, yes. Can you spare it? *(She moves to Maud and takes a cigarette)*

LOTTA *(moving behind the sofa)* How is Martha, Maud?

MAUD. She's fast asleep. She didn't hear a thing.

CORA. Imagine sleeping through all that.

(ESTELLE *takes out a box of matches and lights her own and Cora's cigarettes.* MAUD *takes a cigarette for herself and lights it with her lighter*)

SARITA *(clapping her hands authoritatively)* Light all the candles, François, post-haste. Madame La Marquise will be weary after her journey in the diligence.

DEIRDRE. For the love of God don't let her get her hands on those matches.

(ESTELLE *and* MAUD *hurriedly extinguish their lights and move up* C.
BONITA *enters down the stairs carrying a half bottle of whisky*)

BONITA. Here's the booze, girls. *(She moves to* R *of the card table)*

MAY *(disapprovingly)* Really, Bonita!

(BONITA *pours little nips for everyone.* LOTTA *adds water*)

BONITA *(as she pours)* Miss Archie's having a wonderful time upstairs.

(MAUD *crosses to the card table, takes two drinks, returns up* C, *gives one drink to Estelle, then sits in the tub chair*)

Charging about in her swan-stripes and shouting orders like a Sergeant-Major.

(LOTTA *hands a drink to Deirdre*)

She and Doreen are moving Sarita's things into the room at the end of the passage.

ALMINA. Oh, dear—that's the one next to mine. I shan't sleep a wink, I know I shan't, my heart's pounding as it is. *(She takes a glass and drinks)*

(LOTTA *picks up two drinks, gives one to Cora, then moves to the piano*)

MAUD. Take some bismuth, dear, and a couple of Phensic.

(Bonita *takes a drink for herself.*

Miss Archie *enters on the landing and comes down the stairs. Her pyjamas are sopping wet but she is calmly victorious.*

Doreen *follows her on*)

Miss Archie. That was a close shave and no mistake. Thank God the jolly old extinguisher worked all right.

Cora. It seems to have worked almost too well. You're soaking.

Miss Archie (*moving above the card table*) That was when the damn thing just went off. I was holding it the wrong way round.

Bonita (*handing a drink to Miss Archie*) Have a drop of this, *Mon Colonel,* and slip into something loose before you catch your death.

Miss Archie. Thanks. I could do with a snifter.

Lotta. I think your presence of mind was absolutely splendid, Miss Archie. We're all very grateful to you.

May (*sepulchrally*) Hear, hear!

(*Everyone looks surprised that* May *should even acknowledge anything said by Lotta*)

Lotta (*with a smile*) I'm glad you agree with me, May. (*She crosses slowly above the armchair* LC *to the fireplace, looking May full in the eye*)

(May *meets Lotta's gaze for a moment, then turns her head away.* Maud *rises and crosses to* R *of Lotta*)

Maud (*breaking the silence*) We were wondering if we ought to telephone to Dr Jevons?

Miss Archie. Time enough for that in the morning. (*She lowers her voice and nods towards Sarita*) I've got a pill that'll put her out like a light.

Cora. An unfortunate simile.

(Bonita *sits* R *of the card table*)

Miss Archie (*crossing to* C) Would anyone like a cup of char? It wouldn't take a minute to boil the kettle.

Estelle (*crossing to the card table*) No, thanks, not on top of the whisky. (*She puts her glass on the tray*)

Lotta. Not for me, thank you.

(*There are general murmurs of dissent*)

Miss Archie. In that case, you'd better get back to bed, Doreen.

Doreen. Okay, Miss Archibald.

(Doreen *exits to the kitchen.* Lotta *replaces the fire-stool at the fireplace*)

Cora. I think it's time we all went back to bed.

Miss Archie. I'll just slip out of these and pop on a dressing-gown, then we'll take Sarita up. I shan't be two shakes.

(Miss Archie *exits* L)

Estelle (*taking Almina's hand*) Come on up, Almina. There's no sense in just sitting about.

(Bonita *rises and helps* Almina *to rise*)

Almina. I suppose it's the shock but I'm feeling all trembly.

Estelle (*leading Almina to the stairs*) Well, the shock's over now so there's nothing to feel trembly about any more. Come along.

Almina (*at the foot of the stairs*) Shock's a very dangerous thing. A friend of mine once saw a man run over by a bus in Newcastle and three days later she fell down dead.

Estelle. Come on, dear. It's no use being morbid.

(Estelle *and* Almina *exit slowly up the stairs*)

Sarita. I fell in love with Herbert in Newcastle.

Bonita. Herbert who?

Sarita. My Herbert, of course. We used to go to Whitley Bay on non-matinée days and hold hands and look at the sea.

Maud (*putting her glass on the coffee-table*) I think I'll go up, too. Deirdre, you coming? (*She crosses to the stairs*) Good night, every-body.

Lotta. Good night, Maud.

Bonita. Good night, Maud.

(Maud *exits up the stairs*)

Deirdre (*rising*) All right. (*She crosses to* R *of Sarita and shoots a malevolent glance at her*) A fine moment to be jabbering about hold-ing hands in Whitley Bay when you've just committed arson.

(Deirdre *puts her glass on the coffee-table and exits up the stairs.*
Miss Archie *enters* L, *wearing her dressing-gown and slippers*)

Miss Archie (*moving to* L *of Sarita*) Come along, old dear. (*She helps Sarita to her feet*) Time for Bedfordshire.

Sarita (*with a step towards Cora*) My brother Armand and I were all in all to each other, he the little father, I the tiny mother.

Bonita. Good Lord! *The Scarlet Pimpernel.*

Miss Archie (*leading Sarita to the stairs*) Give me a hand, Bonita.

(Bonita *moves to Sarita and takes her arm*)

Sarita (*shaking off Bonita's hand*) I am sorry if I have done any-thing wrong, but please do not touch me. I cannot bear people to touch me. (*She goes quickly up the stairs*)

Miss Archie (*to Bonita*) Quickly—head her off from going to her own room. I don't want her to see it as it is.

BONITA (*going quickly up the stairs*) I hope you've got that pill handy.

(BONITA *passes above Sarita on the landing and exits.* MISS ARCHIE *goes up the stairs to* R *of Sarita*)

SARITA (*leaning over the rail*) The sea was rather muddy and there was always a wind but there was a freshness in the air and we were in love.

MISS ARCHIE. Come along, old dear.

(SARITA *and* MISS ARCHIE *exit on the landing.* CORA *moves behind the sofa and stands with her back to the others.* MAY *rises and moves towards the armchair* LC)

CORA (*in a muffled voice*) Oh, God! It's intolerable—intolerable.

(MAY *stops and looks at Cora*)

LOTTA (*crossing to* L *of the sofa*) Of course it is, but it's no use allowing yourself to be upset by it. There's nothing to be done.

CORA. I suppose she'll have to be sent away—eventually.

LOTTA. Yes. I suppose she will.

CORA (*turning to Lotta*) What happens when the mind goes like that?

(MAY *moves to the armchair* LC *and sits*)

Does it make it better or worse—living, I mean.

LOTTA. Who knows? More bearable, perhaps. I think Sarita is quite happy.

CORA (*pulling herself together*) I expect she's to be envied, really. At least, she doesn't realize what a bore it is, all this sitting about and waiting. (*She moves up* C, *switches off the wall-bracket* R, *starts up the stairs, but stops halfway and turns*)

(LOTTA *moves to the foot of the stairs*)

Are you coming, May?

MAY. No. I'm going to stay by the fire for a little.

(CORA *goes on to the landing*)

LOTTA (*cheerfully*) So am I.

(CORA *looks at Lotta and May, switches off the landing bracket and exits.* MAY *looks sharply at* LOTTA, *then looks away.* LOTTA *goes to the coffee-table, puts down her glass, then sits on the sofa at the upstage end. There is a long silence.* MAY *picks up her embroidery bag, shoots Lotta another swift look, fumbles in the bag and produces her spectacle case. She gives a little grunt of satisfaction.* LOTTA *sits quietly staring in front of her. The silence continues*)

MAY (*presently*) They were here all the time.

(LOTTA, *without replying, looks enquiringly at May*)

(*She meets Lotta's eyes and forces a wintry little smile*) My glasses. They were here all the time—in my work bag.

LOTTA (*gently*)
> "And frosts were slain and flowers begotten
> And in green underwood and cover
> Blossom by blossom the Spring begins."

MAY (*after a pause*) The fire's nearly out.

LOTTA. There's enough heat left, really. It's not very cold.

MAY (*after a pause*) Were you happy with him?

LOTTA. Yes. I was happy with him until the day he died.

MAY. That's something gained at any rate, isn't it?

LOTTA (*lightly*) He was a monster sometimes, of course. Those black Irish rages.

MAY. Yes. I remember them well. (*She looks curiously at Lotta. Without emotion*) Why did you take him from me?

LOTTA. I didn't. He came to me of his own free will. You must have known that. He wasn't the sort of character that anyone could take from anyone else.

MAY (*dispassionately*) You were prettier than I was.

LOTTA. You know perfectly well that that had nothing to do with it. The spark is struck or it isn't. It's seldom the fault of any one person.

MAY. Any one person can achieve a lot by determination.

LOTTA. Would you like a piece of accurate but rather unpleasant information?

MAY. What do you mean?

LOTTA. There was somebody else.

MAY. Somebody else?

LOTTA. Yes. Between the time he left you and came to me.

MAY. I don't believe it.

LOTTA. It's quite true. Her name was Lavinia—Lavinia Parsons.

MAY (*incredulously*) Not that dreadful girl who played Ophelia with poor old Godfrey?

LOTTA. That's the one.

MAY. Are you telling me this in order to exonerate yourself?

LOTTA (*with a touch of asperity*) No, May. I'm not apologizing to you, you know, nor asking for your forgiveness. I see no reason to exonerate myself. Charles fell in love with me and I fell in love with him and were were married. I have no regrets.

MAY (*dryly*) You are very fortunate. I have—a great many.

LOTTA. Well, don't. It's a waste of time.

MAY (*after a pause*) What became of your first husband—Webster whatever-his-name-was?

LOTTA (*evenly*) His name was Webster Bennet. After our divorce in nineteen twenty-six, he went to Canada and died there a few years later.

May. You had a son, didn't you?

Lotta. Yes, I had a son.

May. Is he alive?

Lotta. Yes. He went to Canada with his father. He is there still. He has had two wives: the first one apparently was a disaster, the second one we'll hope is satisfactory.

May. Does he write to you often?

Lotta. I haven't heard from him for seventeen years.

May (*gruffly*) I'm sorry, Lotta, very sorry.

Lotta. Thank you, that's kind of you. I was unhappy about it for a long time but I'm not any more. He was always his father's boy more than mine, I don't think he ever cared for me much, except of course when he was little.

May (*after a pause*) Why did you come here? Was it absolutely necessary?

Lotta (*looking down*) Yes, absolutely. I have a minute income of two hundred pounds a year and nothing saved; the last two plays I did were failures and—and there was nothing else to be done. Also I found I couldn't learn lines any more—that broke my nerve.

May. That's what really finished me, too. I was always a slow study at the best of times, the strain became intolerable and humiliating, more humiliating even than this.

Lotta. I refuse to consider this humiliating. I think we've earned this honestly, really I do.

May. Perhaps we have, Lotta, perhaps we have.

Lotta (*glancing at the card table*) Bonita's left her bottle of whisky. (*She raises and picks up her glass*) Would you like a sip? (*She moves to the card table*)

May. A very small one.

Lotta (*pouring two drinks*) All right.

May (*ruminatively*) Lavinia Parsons. He must have been mad. (*She puts her spectacles in her bag and hangs the bag on the arm of her chair*)

Lotta (*crossing and handing a drink to May*) She was prettier than you and prettier than me and a great deal younger than both of us.

May (*thoughtfully*) I must buy a bottle of whisky tomorrow in Maidenhead. What is really the best sort?

Lotta. Oh, I don't know. There's "Haig and Haig" and "Black and White"—they're all much of a muchness unless one happens to be a connoisseur, and we're neither of us that.

May (*rising and holding up her glass*) Well, Lotta—we meet again.

Lotta. Yes, May dear, we meet again.

(*They clink glasses*)

Happy days!

May. Happy days!

They drink and then stand quite still for a moment looking at each other. In their eyes there is a glint of tears as—

the Curtain *falls*

SCENE 3

SCENE—*The same. A week later. Afternoon.*

Before the CURTAIN *rises, the music of "Miss Mouse" is heard.*

When the CURTAIN *rises, it is just after lunch on Sunday. The music fades.* CORA *is seated at the desk playing patience.* DEIRDRE *is seated at the downstage end of the sofa reading the "Sunday Times".* BONITA *is seated at the upstage end of the sofa reading the "Sunday Clarion".* MAUD *is seated at the piano playing the Eighteenth Rachmaninov Paganini Variation.* ALMINA *is in the tub chair, reading a newspaper.* ESTELLE *is seated in the armchair up* L, *knitting.* MAY *is seated* LC, *working at her embroidery.* LOTTA *is seated in the easy chair down* L, *reading the "Sunday Clarion".*

LOTTA. You really must listen to this, May, it really is too ghastly. (*She laughs*)

MAY. I have already told you I do not wish to hear a word of it.

LOTTA (*reading*) "Old foes still feuding in the twilight of their lives!" It's in large black letters, May. The first time we've ever been co-starred.

(*All but* MAY *laugh*)

MAY. I can see nothing to laugh at.

LOTTA. It's vulgar and inaccurate and full of treacly sentimentality, I admit, but somehow it isn't as bad as I feared.

MAY. I cannot imagine how it could have been much worse.

LOTTA. It might have been a good deal more vindictive. I wouldn't have been surprised, after Deirdre's little outburst.

DEIRDRE. I said what I had in my heart to say to the fawning, deceitful creature and I don't regret a word of it.

CORA. Deirdre can make anything sound like a *Lyceum* melodrama.

DEIRDRE. And what's wrong with that, I should like to know? The *Lyceum* melodrama at least gave you your money's worth. An honest bit of blood and thunder's a lot more healthy and entertaining than all this modern creeping about in the pitch dark and complaining.

MAY. For once I am in complete agreement with Deirdre.

DEIRDRE. The skies will fall, I shouldn't wonder.

BONITA (*poring over her paper*) She's even dragged poor old

Osgood in. It's lower down in the column after the bit about us all sitting in the garden at dusk listening to the rooks cawing and wistfully remembering our former triumphs.

CORA. Sitting in the garden at dusk, indeed! We should be eaten alive.

LOTTA. She seemed quite a well-educated young woman. It's curious that she should write so abominably.

MAY. No other sort of writing would be accepted by that horrible rag. There is no elegance, dignity or reticence left. "Milton, thou should'st be living at this hour—England hath need of thee."

CORA (*laconically*) Curtain!

LOTTA (*looking at her paper*) Oh, really! Listen to this (*She reads*) "I wonder if we ordinary people realize how much we owe to these old faithful servants of the public, wearily playing out the last act of their lives, all passion spent, all glamour gone, unwanted and forgotten, just waiting—waiting in "The Wings"".

BONITA. That would make a wonderful number.

MAUD. I've got it. (*She plays a few chords and sings*)

> Waiting in the Wings,
> Waiting in the Wings—

(BONITA *rises and moves to the piano.* ESTELLE *rises*)

> Older than God,
> On we plod,
> Waiting in the Wings.

BONITA (*joining in*)
> Hopping about the garden,
> Like a lot of Douglas Byngs,

(ALMINA *rises. She and* ESTELLE *do a little dance to the last line.*
OSGOOD *enters timidly from the hall, carrying his usual bunch of violets*)

MAUD }
BONITA } (*together; with a bravura finish*)

> Waiting, waiting, waiting in the Wings.

(*They all applaud and laugh*)

OSGOOD. Good afternoon. I hope I'm not interrupting anything?

(ESTELLE *and* ALMINA *subside rather sheepishly into their chairs*)

LOTTA. Of course you're not, we're just feeling rather skittish.

OSGOOD. The front door was on the latch so I didn't bother to ring the bell.

BONITA. Quite right. You're one of the family, anyhow. (*She crosses to the french windows*)

Osgood (*moving to the stairs*) How kind of you to say that, how very kind. I suppose it will be all right if I go straight up?

Maud. I'm sure it will—I'll call Miss Archie if you like.

Osgood. No—no—please don't trouble. I know the way. (*He goes up to the landing*) There's such a nice article about all of you in the *Sunday Clarion*. I read it in the train coming down—it almost brought tears to my eyes, so sensitively written, most touching —most touching.

(Osgood *exits on the landing*)

May. The poor man must be out of his mind.

Lotta. An honest reaction from an ordinary member of the public.

Bonita. I give up.

Cora. It only goes to prove that we are all far too touchy.

(*The sound of a motor-cycle horn is heard off*)

Here's Perry.

Lotta. Poor boy, I feel so sorry for him.

May. Personally, I find it hard to forgive him for unleashing all this vulgarity on our heads.

Deirdre. Then it's shame you should be feeling, May Davenport.

Estelle (*rising*) Do you think he's come to say "good-bye"?

Maud (*rising*) Good-bye! Oh, how awful!

Estelle (*moving to* R *of May*) Whatever should we do without him?

Bonita. I shouldn't. I'd leave.

Cora. And where would you go, may I ask?

Bonita (*crossing to the sofa*) I'd go and live with my horrible niece in Penge. (*She sits on the sofa at the upstage end*)

Deirdre. We'd all go on strike.

Estelle (*crossing to the fireplace*) Suppose this is the last time we shall ever see him—I can't bear it.

Lotta. I think we had all better keep quite calm until Perry can tell us exactly what happened.

(Perry *enters from the hall. His usual cheerfulness is not apparent*)

Perry. Hullo, everybody.

Maud. Oh, Perry! (*She goes impulsively and kisses him*)

(Estelle *moves above the armchair* LC)

Perry. I see that one of you has forgiven me at least.

Lotta. Nonsense! We've all forgiven you ages ago, except May, and she's only holding out so that you can make an extra fuss of her.

May. Really, Lotta! How can you say such things!

PERRY (*moving down* R *to* L *of Cora*) I suppose you've all read it?
CORA. We certainly have.
PERRY (*crossing below the sofa to* LC) It's no use me saying I'm sorry any more, is it? I mean—I did write and try to explain . . .
LOTTA. It was a very nice letter, Perry. Miss Archie read it out to us. (*She holds out her hand*)

(PERRY *moves and takes Lotta's hand*)

CORA (*rising and turning*) But that was before the special meeting.

(MAUD *sits on the upstage arm of the sofa*)

What happened? (*She sits below the card table*)
PERRY. Exactly what I expected would happen.
BONITA. Oh, Perry!
PERRY. It was hell.
ESTELLE (*wretchedly*) Oh, poor Perry. (*She moves to* R *of Perry*) It was all my fault. I shall never forgive myself—never.
MAUD. What happened exactly, Perry? Tell us.
BONITA. For Heaven's sake, Perry.

(ESTELLE, *sniffing, moves to the chair up* L *and sits*)

PERRY. Oh, they all flew at me and Boodie Nethersole said a lot about me exceeding my duties and assuming responsibilities that I had no right to assume.
BONITA. Silly bitch!
MAY. Bonita—please!
LOTTA. Go on, Perry.
PERRY. Dame Maggie had already telephoned to the editor of the *Clarion* to have Zelda's piece stopped but he flatly refused. Then after a lot more talk they told me that I should have to go. I was sacked.

(*There is general reaction with exclamations of horror and dismay from everyone*)

LOTTA. Oh, Perry, I really am most distressed. We all are.
PERRY (*with the suspicion of a twinkle in his eye*) Even May?
MAY (*busy with her embroidery*) I'm sure I hope it will be a lesson to you in the future.
LOTTA. Really, May. I think you are being unnecessarily disagreeable.
DEIRDRE. And what would you expect from granite but a heart of stone?
LOTTA (*crossly*) Do be quiet, Deirdre.
DEIRDRE (*flaring up*) And why should I be quiet? The poor lad loses his job. And on top of that he's talked to by May Davenport as though he were a juvenile delinquent hauled up before the bar of justice for rape and bloody murder.

BONITA ⎤   ⎧Murder! I could murder the lot of them.
MAUD   ⎬ (*together*) ⎨Oh, Perry, whatever will you do?
ESTELLE⎦   ⎨It's terrible. (*She rises and crosses to Almina*)
                        ⎩It's simply terrible.

PERRY (*crossing to Bonita*) Just a moment, everybody, please. I haven't quite finished my story.

LOTTA (*quickly sensing a change in his tone*) Go on, then, Perry. Finish it.

PERRY (*enjoying himself*) There was another meeting called yesterday. A much smaller one. Dame Maggie was in the chair and Boodie, thank God, was playing her matinée.

LOTTA. I hope I've guessed what happened—go on.

PERRY. The resolution of Thursday's meeting, by some oversight, had not been minuted. And so, after rather a kind little lecture, I was reinstated.

(*There are universal exclamations of delight and relief.* MAUD *rises, goes to Perry and flings her arms around him*)

MAUD. Hurray!

LOTTA. How perfectly splendid!

PERRY. And would you all like to know why I was reinstated?

ALL (*ad lib.*) Yes.

PERRY. Why there was such a sudden change in the weather?

MAY (*in authoritative tones*) Perry! I absolutely forbid you to say another word.

PERRY. Just allow me five. (*He crosses to May*) Thank you, dear, dear May.

(PERRY *kisses May warmly on her cheek, then crosses and exits* L. *There is a stunned silence.* MAUD *sits on the upstage arm of the sofa*)

BONITA (*presently*) Well, I'll be damned!

DEIRDRE. What in the name of the Blessed Saints did he do that for?

LOTTA. You've been very sly, May. I'm surprised at you. Did you write to Maggie?

MAY. I'd prefer not to discuss it.

BONITA. You must tell us, you really must—please, May.

MAY. I telephoned to Dame Maggie from Miss Archie's office on Thursday evening while you were all at supper. I explained that the whole thing had been a foolish mistake on Perry's part and that he was too important to all of us to be summarily dismissed for such a trivial misdemeanour. I added that we were all prepared to write strong letters of protest to the committee.

DEIRDRE. Well, blow me down and bury me bones if that's not the biggest surprise I've ever had in my life. Hats off to you, May Davenport.

MAY. Once and for all, will you stop calling me "May Davenport".

(*The front-door bell rings*)

MAUD. Who's that, I wonder?

CORA (*rising and moving down* R) Dr Jevons, I expect.

LOTTA (*rising and moving to the fireplace; stricken*) Of course, yes.
I'd quite forgotten. How horrid.

(DOREEN *enters from the kitchen and exits* R *in the hall*)

ALMINA. I'd forgotten, too, for the moment, what with the
Clarion article and Perry arriving and everything.

(*The front door is heard to slam*)

Poor old love. (*She sighs*) I suppose it's all for the best, really.

(DOREEN *enters the hall from* R.
      DR JEVONS *follows her on. He is a pleasant-looking young man
in the thirties*)

DR JEVONS (*crossing to* C) Good afternoon, ladies.

(DOREEN *exits to the kitchen*)

ALL (*ad lib.*) Good afternoon, Dr Jevons.

DR JEVONS. Is Miss Archie in her office?

LOTTA. No, she's upstairs. It's not an ambulance, is it?

DR JEVONS. No, no—nothing like that. Just my old Hillman.
I'm driving her myself.

LOTTA. How nice of you. I'm so glad.

DR JEVONS. I'll go up. (*He goes to the stairs, pauses, then turns*)
May I suggest something—without appearing to be unduly
officious?

MAY. Of course, Doctor. What is it?

DR JEVONS. I think it would be advisable if no "good-byes"
were said or implied. Just behave ordinarily, as though nothing
had happened.

LOTTA. It is absolutely necessary for her to go—to go away,
isn't it?

DR JEVONS. In my opinion, yes, but I do assure you there is
nothing to worry about. She will be well and most kindly taken
care of, and never made to feel that she is in any way—er—out of
line.

LOTTA. Thank you. I'm so glad.

(DR JEVONS *exits up the stairs. There is a long silence*)

BONITA. I wonder how he can be so certain—that there's
nothing to worry about, I mean?

LOTTA. There is no absolute certainty, I suppose. But he is a
good doctor and a sensible, kindly man. I'd be inclined to trust
his word.

CORA. In any case there really isn't any alternative.

MAUD. No, I suppose not, but it does seem awful, somehow.

MAY (*firmly*) Of course there's no alternative. She obviously must go somewhere where she can be under proper supervision, somewhere where she isn't dangerous to anyone else.

BONITA. The poor old duck didn't mean to be dangerous.

MAY. I am not suggesting that she did, Bonita. But the fact remains—she was.

(PERRY *enters* L)

PERRY. Was that the doctor?

ESTELLE. Yes. He's gone up.

PERRY (*crossing to* C) Does she know that she is being sent to—being sent away?

CORA. Miss Archie explained to her tactfully this morning that she was going to stay with some new friends, but she didn't seem to take it in.

PERRY. Oh, poor old girl. I do hope she won't mind.

LOTTA. That's what haunts me, the idea of waking up in strange surroundings and being suddenly lonely and afraid.

MAUD (*rising and moving to the piano stool*) Oh, don't—I can't bear it. (*She sits*)

(PERRY *goes to Maud, pats her hand, then goes up the stairs to the landing*)

DEIRDRE. An aunt of mine went off her head when I was a wee girl, I remember it well. There was no shilly-shallying about in those days. They came for her in the middle of Sunday dinner and hauled her off to the asylum like a sack of potatoes.

LOTTA. Oh, Deirdre, really!

PERRY (*listening*) I think they're coming down now. (*He comes down the stairs*)

ESTELLE (*emotionally*) Oh, dear—I don't think I can bear it. (*She moves and stands above the sofa*) I shall only cry and make a fool of myself. (*She turns to go*)

CORA. Stay where you are. The doctor said we were to behave as though nothing had happened.

(ESTELLE *crosses to the firestool and sits*)

LOTTA. We'd better talk, I think.

BONITA (*miserably*) I can't think of anything to say. (*She picks up a book from the coffee-table*)

LOTTA. Play the piano, Maud. Play anything that comes into your head.

MAUD. Oh, no—I couldn't.

LOTTA. Please—just to cover up the silence—quickly. (*She sits in the easy chair down* L *and reads her paper*)

MAUD. All right. (*She plays the Nocturne in F sharp major by Chopin*)

(CORA *sits at the desk and plays patience.* DEIRDRE, BONITA *and* ALMINA *read books and papers.*

MISS ARCHIE, SARITA *and* DR JEVONS *enter on the landing.* MISS ARCHIE *carries a suitcase.* SARITA *is in a grey coat and skirt and wears a small hat.* MISS ARCHIE *comes down the stairs.* SARITA *stops and looks over the rail.* DR JEVONS *stands* L *of Sarita*)

SARITA. What a charming hotel. It has quite an atmosphere of home, hasn't it?

MISS ARCHIE. That's right, dear. Come along.

SARITA (*listening to Maud playing and nodding her head in time to the music*) I remember that tune—it's Chopin, isn't it?

MAUD (*still playing; rather tremulously*) Yes, dear—it's Chopin.

SARITA. I made an exit to it in *Lady Mary's Secret* many, many years ago. (*She smiles at Dr Jevons*) Long before your day, young man. (*She moves to the top of the stairs*)

(*The others slowly turn to listen and watch Sarita*)

It was a lovely long exit and I wore a white evening dress, and just as I got to the door I turned slowly and threw a red rose to my leading man. (*She comes down the stairs*)

(DR JEVONS *moves to the top of the stairs*)

It was only a property rose, of course, and he didn't always catch it, but it always brought the house down.

(PERRY *offers his arm to* SARITA, *but she crosses to* C.

MISS ARCHIE *exits* R *in the hall.* DR JEVONS *comes down the stairs*)

Au revoir, my dears. I won't say "good-bye" because it is so unlucky. It has been such a really lovely engagement. Good luck to you all.

SARITA *turns to* PERRY *who moves to her and leads her off* R *in the hall.*

DR JEVONS *follows them off. The others all watch, except* MAUD *who gallantly continues to play as—*

the CURTAIN *falls*

C

ACT III

Scene i

SCENE—*The same. The evening of Christmas Day.*
There is a slight re-arrangement of the furniture. The sofa is now R,
the card table is RC *and the coffee-table* LC. *The upright chairs from the
card table have been removed.*

Before the CURTAIN *rises, the music of "Oh, Mr Kaiser" is heard.*

When the CURTAIN *rises, the room is empty. It is about nine-thirty p.m.
The room shows signs of festivity. There are some paper decorations
here and there, and above the fireplace. A Christmas tree with lights
stands by the french windows. The wall-brackets are not on, but the
other lights are lit. A cheerful fire burns in the grate. The music fades.*
DOREEN *enters from the kitchen and switches on the wall-brackets* R.
She then collects discarded paper wrappings from the piano. MISS
ARCHIE *enters* R *in the hall. She is resplendent in A.T.S. uniform,
but wears a rather coquettish paper cap. A buzz of conversation and
laughter is heard from the dining-room.*

MISS ARCHIE (*collecting wrapping papers from the sofa*) You can
leave all that mess till tomorrow, Doreen.

(DOREEN *collects papers from the floor by the Christmas tree*)

Go and get the coffee and then cut along home to your family—
you've had quite a day. (*She collects an empty cracker box and some
wrappings from the card table*)

DOREEN (*moving*) Okay, Miss Archie—thanks.

MISS ARCHIE (*moving to Doreen and handing her the box, etc.*) There
are two boxes of crackers left over—you can take them to your
little brother.

DOREEN. Thanks ever so.

MISS ARCHIE (*crossing to* L) And wish him jolly good hols, jolly
good term and jolly good luck with his eleven plus. (*She switches
on the wall-brackets* L)

DOREEN. He's as bright as a button, really. If it wasn't for his
impediment.

MISS ARCHIE (*moving to the coffee-table*) Good Lord—what's a
stutter? (*She collects wrappings, etc. from the coffee-table and gives them
to Doreen*) Look at that corporal clerk of mine—Betty Something
—worst stutter I ever heard—and where is she now?

DOREEN. I couldn't say, Miss Archibald.

MISS ARCHIE. Right up with the top brass at Peter Jones.

(*The front-door bell rings*)

62

Now, who the devil can that be at this time of night? Run and see, there's a good girl. I'll take these. (*She relieves Doreen of the wrappings*)

(Miss Archie *exits to the kitchen.*
Doreen *exits* R *in the hall.*
Zelda *enters* R *in the hall.* Doreen *follows her on.* Zelda, *dressed for the evening, is wearing black corduroy trousers, a black velvet jacket, a white shirt and a red scarf. She is carrying a large and obviously heavy package which she deposits on the card table*)

Doreen. I'll tell Miss Archie you're here.
Zelda. Thank you. (*She moves* C)

(Doreen *exits to the kitchen*)

Doreen (*off*) Someone to see you, Miss Archibald.

(Miss Archie *enters from the kitchen*)

Miss Archie (*nonplussed*) Oh!
Zelda. Good evening.
Miss Archie (*moving to* L *of the card table; awkwardly*) I didn't realize who it was—I mean, Doreen didn't say . . .
Zelda. Happy Christmas.
Miss Archie (*with an anxious glance towards the dining-room*) The same to you.
Zelda. I've been at a party in Maidenhead and I'm on my way back to London. I thought I'd call in for a moment, with a peace offering.
Miss Archie. Peace offering?
Zelda. That's it—on the table. It's a case of champagne.
Miss Archie (*moving to* R *of the card table*) Champagne—Good Lord! I really don't think that . . .
Zelda. I gather that I am still in the dog house?
Miss Archie. Well, Miss Fenwick—I wouldn't exactly say that—but of course they were a bit upset at the time, and it's no use saying they weren't.
Zelda (*moving to* L *of the card table*) Please don't be embarrassed. I'm only staying for a moment. You needn't even say I've been here if you don't want to. You can pretend the champagne was just left at the door. I hasten to add that I am not here in a professional capacity, for once. It's just that I had rather a guilty conscience.
Miss Archie. I see.
Zelda. Not about what I wrote, please don't misunderstand me, that was part of my job, but because I didn't keep my word.
Miss Archie. I don't quite know what you mean.
Zelda. I promised Perry I'd make an appeal on my T.V. programme.
Miss Archie. Oh, that—yes, I remember.

ZELDA. But the T.V. people were against it, so was my editor, so—so I gave in.

MISS ARCHIE. Please don't worry any more about it. It's all over and forgotten. (*She moves towards the desk*) Can I offer you a drink?

ZELDA. No, thanks, I must go. I've got a friend outside in the car. (*She takes an envelope from her pocket and moves down* RC) My boss asked me to give you this—for "The Wings".

MISS ARCHIE. Your boss?

ZELDA. His Lordship. He's a barking old tyrant but he is in mortal dread of Hell's fire and so he occasionally likes to make a gesture. It may be a form of spiritual insurance or it may even be genuine kindness, with him it's difficult to tell. At any rate—this is it. (*She hands the envelope to Miss Archie*)

(MISS ARCHIE *opens the envelope and extracts a cheque*)

MISS ARCHIE. Good God! Two thousand pounds!

ZELDA. It's for the Solarium.

MISS ARCHIE. I can't believe it.

ZELDA. There are no strings attached. It's a private donation for a specific purpose, so see that the committee don't use it for anything else. (*She moves up* RC) I'll be getting along now. (*She stops and turns*) Give my love to the inmates, even that old Irish battleaxe.

MISS ARCHIE. Please stay a minute.

ZELDA. No, I think I'd better go.

MISS ARCHIE. At least give them a chance to say thank you.

ZELDA (*moving down* RC) I don't want them to say thank you, they have to say thank you every day of their lives; they must be sick to death of it. I'm off.

MISS ARCHIE. Perhaps you'll let me say it, then—on their behalf.

ZELDA (*with a smile*) All right—fire away.

MISS ARCHIE (*moving to Zelda; obviously moved but trying to conceal it*) Thank you. (*She wrings Zelda's hand*)

ZELDA. Be careful—I need my hand to drive the car. (*She backs up* RC, *flexing her fingers*)

MISS ARCHIE (*huskily*) Sorry.

ZELDA. You know, curiously enough, that paper hat is rather becoming. (*She smiles*) Good night, Colonel.

(ZELDA *salutes and exits* R *in the hall.* MISS ARCHIE *stands quite still for a moment staring at the cheque, then replaces it in the envelope, crosses and puts it on the mantelpiece.*

DOREEN *enters from the kitchen staggering under the weight of a large tray of coffee*)

DOREEN. Do they want it in the dining-room, or in here?

MISS ARCHIE. In here—put it on the table.

DOREEN. Okay, Miss Archie. (*She puts the tray on the coffee-table*) Will that be all?

MISS ARCHIE. Yes, Doreen, that'll be all.

DOREEN. Ta ever so for the brooch—it's smashing.

MISS ARCHIE. I'm glad you like it.

DOREEN. Well—bye-bye for now.

MISS ARCHIE. Bye-bye for now.

(DOREEN *exits to the kitchen.*

LOTTA, MAY, OSGOOD *and* PERRY *enter from the hall.* OSGOOD *and* PERRY *are wearing dinner jackets.*

ALMINA, MAUD, ESTELLE, DEIRDRE, CORA *and* BONITA *follow them on. They are all, more or less, in evening-dress and most of them still have on paper caps.* MAY *crosses to the armchair* LC *and sits.* LOTTA *stands above the card table.* MAUD *and* PERRY *stand up* RC, *near the piano.* DEIRDRE *stands* R *of* CORA *up* LC. ESTELLE *and* BONITA *cross to the coffee-table*)

LOTTA. The turkey was delicious, Miss Archie, in fact the whole dinner was perfect.

(OSGOOD *leads* ALMINA *to the easy chair down* L)

ALMINA. It will take me at least three days to get over it. (*She sits*)

LOTTA. We really ought to say thank you to Mrs Blake—is she still here?

MISS ARCHIE. No, she's gone home.

LOTTA. We must remember in the morning.

BONITA. Coffee everybody?

ALMINA. Not for me, I shouldn't sleep a wink.

(ESTELLE *takes two cups of coffee, gives one to Lotta, then stands at the upstage end of the sofa.* OSGOOD *gives a cup of coffee to May, takes one for himself, then sits on the fire-stool.* BONITA *gives cups of coffee to Maud and Perry, then to Cora and Deirdre, takes one for herself and crosses to Maud*)

PERRY (*seeing the package on the card table*) Hullo—what's this?

MISS ARCHIE. It's a case of champagne.

BONITA. A *case* of champagne! Somebody must have gone mad.

MAY. Where on earth did it come from?

MISS ARCHIE. I expect you'll be angry when I tell you.

MAY. Why?

(ESTELLE *sits on the sofa at the upstage end*)

MISS ARCHIE. Zelda Fenwick brought it—a few minutes ago —she was on her way up to London and she just dropped in—to wish you all a happy Christmas.

ESTELLE. Zelda Fenwick—good heavens!

MISS ARCHIE. She said it was a peace offering.

Cora. Are we to be photographed drinking it?

Miss Archie (*collecting a cup of coffee*) No. There were no ulterior motives. (*She moves to the fireplace*) She meant it kindly—I assure you she did.

Perry. I think it was very decent of her.

Deirdre (*moving* c) Send it back—we don't want to be beholden to her.

Lotta. I think that would be ungracious.

Deirdre. Champagne, indeed—(*she crosses to the sofa and sits at the downstage end*) for a lot of defeated, miserable old crones.

Lotta. We are *not* defeated, miserable old crones, Deirdre. We are well cared for, very comfortable and we have just enjoyed a most excellent Christmas dinner. I think it was extremely generous of Miss Fenwick to bring us a case of champagne and I propose that we open a bottle immediately and drink her health.

Bonita. Hear, hear!

Miss Archie. Miss Fenwick brought something else, too. (*She takes the envelope from the mantelpiece, crosses to* c *and faces up stage*) It's this.

Maud. What is it?

Miss Archie. A present to "The Wings" from her boss Lord Charkley. It's a cheque for two thousand pounds, for the Solarium.

(*There is a stunned silence*)

Perry. Well, I'll be damned!

Cora (*incredulously*) Two thousand pounds!

Estelle (*rising*) It can't be true—(*she bursts into tears*) it can't be true!

(Perry *runs to Miss Archie, takes the cheque from the envelope and stares at it*)

Perry (*awe-stricken*) It is true—two thousand bloody pounds. (*He rushes around and shows the cheque to Deirdre, Lotta, Estelle and Bonita*)

(Miss Archie *moves to* l *of the coffee-table.* Cora *moves up* l *of the coffee-table and puts down her cup*)

May (*with routine disapproval*) Really, Perry!

Cora. Where's the catch in it? There must be a catch somewhere.

Miss Archie. She said that there were no strings attached, that it was a private donation and that I was to inform the committee that it was for the Solarium and nothing else.

Perry (*devoutly*) Boodie Nethersole thou should'st be with us at this hour. (*He kisses the cheque, crosses to Miss Archie and returns it to her*)

(Miss Archie *puts the cheque on the mantelpiece*)

BONITA (*moving above the coffee-table*) To hell with Boodie Nethersole—to hell with the committee—this is the most wonderful thing that ever happened.

MAY. I don't think you should say "to hell with the committee", Bonita, even in fun. They do their best and they *did* send all of us those pretty little powder compacts.

LOTTA (*laughing*) Oh, May!

MISS ARCHIE (*picking up the tray*) Come on, Perry my lad— bring that case of booze into the kitchen and let's bash it open.

(BONITA *and* MAUD *put their cups on the tray*)

PERRY. Right!

(PERRY *picks up the package and exits to the kitchen.* MAUD *sits on the piano stool.* LOTTA *moves to the desk and puts her cup on it*)

MISS ARCHIE. I'm afraid we'll have to use tumblers—there aren't any champagne glasses.

(MISS ARCHIE *exits to the kitchen.*
OSGOOD *rises, takes May's cup and exits to the kitchen*)

CORA (*moving to R of May*) Whoever heard of a home for defeated old crones without champagne glasses!

(*All laugh except* ESTELLE *who bursts into tears.* BONITA *crosses to the fire-stool and sits*)

ESTELLE (*moving to L of the card table*) Oh, I am so glad—so very, very glad.

CORA. Cheer up, dear—there really isn't anything to cry about.

ESTELLE. I can't help it—I always cry when something nice happens.

(CORA *goes to the tub chair and sits.* LOTTA *sits on the desk chair*)

DEIRDRE. Don't waste your foolish tears on a scrap of happiness, Estelle. Save 'em until you need 'em, and you will, one of these fine days, mark my words.

(ESTELLE *goes to the Christmas tree*)

MAY (*with a note of irritation*) I sometimes wonder, Deirdre, if you ever believe *anything* you say.

DEIRDRE (*rising belligerently*) And what might you be meaning by that?

MAY. I would like to know what inspires your continual harping on misery and age and the imminence of death. Are you so afraid of it? Are you whistling in the dark?

DEIRDRE (*crossing to* C) I've never been afraid of anyone or anything, May Davenport, since the day I was born.

MAY. In that case it would be kinder to spare the feelings of those who are less courageous.

DEIRDRE. The Blessed Lord will gather me to His bosom when my time comes and that'll be that.

MAY. Presumably the Blessed Lord will gather us all to His bosom when our time comes. I see no reason to suppose that you have an exclusive monopoly. In the meantime I suggest that you allow us to endure our remaining years as cheerfully as possible.

BONITA. Hurray!

DEIRDRE. That's right—take sides against me, all of you—just because I'm old and weary and a foreigner among you. (*She moves to the sofa*)

CORA. You've got more vitality than all of us put together, so be quiet and stop overacting.

DEIRDRE. Overacting, now, am I?

MAY (*majestically*) Yes, Deirdre, you are, and you always did.

(DEIRDRE *sits on the sofa at the downstage end and removes her paper cap.* LOTTA *rises and soothes her*)

BONITA. Never mind about all that now. Let's stop arguing—after all, it is Christmas.

(*The sound of a champagne cork popping is heard off in the kitchen*)

(*She listens*) I don't think I've heard that sound since they turned *Daly's* into a cinema.

(MISS ARCHIE *enters from the kitchen carrying a tray of tumblers.*
PERRY *enters from the kitchen carrying two opened bottles of champagne. He puts one bottle on the coffee-table.* MISS ARCHIE *moves down* R *with the tray.* LOTTA *and* DEIRDRE *take glasses.* MAUD *rises, goes to Miss Archie, takes two glasses and moves up* C. ESTELLE *crosses to Maud and takes one glass from her.*
OSGOOD *enters from the kitchen*)

ALMINA. This will be the death of me, I know it will, on top of all that brandy sauce.

CORA. I hope it's a good year.

PERRY (*looking at the bottle*) Bollinger nineteen thirty-eight.

CORA (*gloomily*) Never mind.

(PERRY *moves around filling the glasses, starting with Maud*)

MAUD. Only a drop for me—really.

(MISS ARCHIE *gives glasses to Cora and May, then moves to* BONITA *who takes two glasses and gives one to Almina*)

OSGOOD (*moving down* RC) Miss Archie, do you think it would be all right if I took a little sip up to Martha?

(MISS ARCHIE *crosses to Osgood*)

I think it would please her.

MISS ARCHIE. Of course—damned good idea. Perry.

(PERRY *moves to Miss Archie and pours champagne into two glasses*)

OSGOOD (*taking the two glasses*) Thank you. She won't be asleep, will she?

MISS ARCHIE. She may be dozing, but she never really settles down for the night before eleven.

(PERRY *pours champagne for Bonita and Almina*)

OSGOOD (*moving to the stairs*) If she is, I'll wake her gently. A little unexpected treat never hurt anyone.

(OSGOOD *exits up the stairs*. PERRY *pours champagne for May and Cora*. MISS ARCHIE *puts the tray on the coffee-table and pours champagne into two glasses*)

BONITA. You know, that man breaks my heart, he really does.

(PERRY *crosses and pours champagne for Lotta and Deirdre*. MAUD *moves to the piano*)

Fancy anyone loving anyone as much as that, over all those years.

MAY (*splendidly*)
             "Love alters not with his brief hours and weeks
             But bears it out even to the edge of doom."

DEIRDRE. Who's harping on death, now, I should like to know?

MAY (*briskly*) William Shakespeare.

DEIRDRE (*with a snort*) I might have known it.

MAY. An unlikely contingency.

(PERRY *puts his bottle on the card table*. MISS ARCHIE *hands a glass of champagne to Perry*)

PERRY. I propose we drink a toast to Zelda Fenwick and Lord Charkley. Will those in favour raise their glasses.

(ALMINA, BONITA *and* CORA *rise*)

CORA. I suppose it's the least we can do really.

(MAY *rises. They all raise their glasses and toast Zelda Fenwick and Lord Charkley*. MAUD *sits at the piano and bangs out* "For they are jolly good fellows". *Everybody joins in and sings. They finish with a flourish and applaud and laugh*. MAUD *continues to play softly through the ensuing dialogue*.

     MISS ARCHIE *picks up Perry's empty bottle and exits to the kitchen*)

PERRY (*picking up the second bottle*) Come on, Bonita, there's plenty more in the kitchen.

BONITA (*crossing to Perry*) Certainly. I shall have a hangover in the morning but who cares.

(Perry *pours champagne for Bonita, then goes round refilling the other glasses*)

Perry. Come on—a little of what you fancy does you good.

Almina. I don't know *what* Dr Jevons would say. (*She resumes her seat*)

Bonita (*meditatively*) There's always something glamorous about champagne, isn't there? I wonder why?

Deirdre. Because it's a devil's brew and very expensive.

Almina. When I was at the *Gaiety* with Millie James she used to have a magnum in her dressing-room every night. That was in nineteen hundred and four.

May. Poor Millie. The results were only too apparent in nineteen hundred and five. (*She resumes her seat*)

(Bonita *crosses to the fireplace.* Lotta *sits* c *of the sofa.* Cora *sits in the tub chair.* Estelle *moves the armchair up* l *and sits near* Cora.

Miss Archie *enters from the kitchen with a new bottle of champagne.* Perry *puts the second empty bottle on the card table.* Maud *breaks into song. As she sings,* Perry *bows to* Miss Archie, *puts his arm around her waist and waltzes with her*)

"CHAMPAGNE"

Maud.   Champagne—Champagne—Champagne,
So sublime, so divine, so profane.
It fizzes and bubbles,
And banishes troubles,
Champagne—champagne—champagne.

(Perry *and* Miss Archie *finish at the foot of the stairs. There is* ᵀ *general laughter.* Perry *takes the bottle from Miss Archie and keeps it*)

Bonita. That's a common little lyric if ever I heard one. (*She sits on the fire-stool*)

Maud (*rising*) It's the waltz from *Miss Mouse*. Poor Dolly Drexell sang it at the end of the second act; she had a big head-dress of ostrich feathers and they kept getting into her mouth.

(Perry *moves down* r *and sits on the desk chair.* Miss Archie *sits on the stairs*)

Lotta. Play the other one, Maudie—the one I like, about little bits of cheese.

Maud (*sitting at the piano*) Oh, dear—I can't remember much of it—wait a minute (*She pauses for a second and then plays a few chords and sings*)

"MISS MOUSE"

Maud.   Won't you come and live in my house—Miss Mouse?

Now, you all have to repeat "Miss Mouse"—let's start again.
(*She sings*)

MAUD.   Won't you come and live in my house—Miss Mouse?
ALL (*singing*)
                Miss Mouse.
MAUD.   It's as sweet as any apple-pie house—Miss Mouse.
ALL.   Miss Mouse.
MAUD.   I will give you honey from the bees,
        Bread and milk and lovely bits of cheese.
        Please, please, please, please, please, please, please,
        Come and live in my house—

(*Spoken*) Altogether.

ALL.   Come and live in my house—
MAUD.   Come and live in my house—
ALL.   Miss Mouse.

        (*Everyone laughs and applauds*)

LOTTA (*laughing*) That really is the most idiotic song I ever
heard.
MAUD. Come on, Bonita—*Over the Hill I'll Find You.*
BONITA. Good God, no—it's too long ago—I couldn't.
MAUD. Come on—I'll prompt you.

        (BONITA *rises and crosses to the piano.* MAUD *plays some intro-
ductory chords.* BONITA *sings in a husky, uncertain voice*)

                "OVER THE HILL"

BONITA.   Over the hill I'll find you
          There by the murmuring stream—

MAUD (*prompting*) "And the bird in the woods . . ."

BONITA.   And the bird in the woods behind you
          Will echo our secret dream.
          There in the twilight waiting,
          Gentle, serene and still,
          All the cares of the day
          Will be banished away
          When I find you, over the hill,
          When I find you, over the hill.

        (*Everyone applauds*)

DEIRDRE. Sentimental poppycock!
MAY. The words are a little sugary but it's a very pretty tune.
BONITA. That'll go better second house. (*She crosses to the
footstool and sits*)
MAUD (*to Perry*) What was that number you did in *Two's a
Crowd,* Perry?
    c**

PERRY. Oh, no, Maudie, I couldn't—I couldn't, really—I'd dry up.

(MISS ARCHIE *rises, moves to Perry, draws him to his feet, pulls him to the piano, then stands behind the sofa. There are general exclamations of encouragement*)

BONITA. Come on, dear, don't be coy, you're among friends. Play it, Maudie.

(MAUD *plays the introduction to "Come The Wild, Wild Weather"*)

PERRY. No—that's too high—can you take it down a bit?

(MAUD *plays the introduction again.* PERRY *sings the number gently and very sweetly*)

"COME THE WILD, WILD WEATHER"

PERRY (*singing*)
>Come the wild, wild weather,
>Come the wind, come the rain.
>Come the little white flakes of snow,
>Come the joy, come the pain,
>We shall still be together
>When our life story ends,
>For wherever we chance to go
>We shall always be friends.
>We may find while we're travelling through the years,
>Moments of joy and love and happiness,
>Reason for grief, reason for tears.
>Come the wild, wild weather,
>If we've lost or we've won,
>We'll remember these words we say
>Till our story is done.
>
>Time may hold in store for us,
>Glory or defeat,
>Maybe never more for us
>Life will seem so sweet.
>Time will change so many things
>Tides will ebb and flow,
>But wherever fate may lead us,
>Always we shall know.
>
>Come the wild, wild weather,
>Come the wind, come the rain,
>Come the little white flakes of snow,
>Come the joy, come the pain,
>We shall still be together
>When our life story ends,
>For wherever we chance to go

We shall always be friends.
We may find while we're travelling through the years,
Moments of joy and love and happiness,
Reason for grief, reason for tears.
Come the wild, wild weather,
If we've lost or we've won,
We'll remember these words we say
Till our story is done.
We'll remember these words we say,
Till our story is over and done
Till our story is over and done.

(*At the end of the number,* May *rises, crosses to Perry and kisses him*)

May. That was charming, dear boy—really charming.
Deirdre (*to Maud*) Play something larky, for the love of Heaven —you'll have us all crying our eyes out in a minute.
May. An Irish jig, perhaps?
Deirdre (*rising*) And what's wrong with that, I should like to know.

(Maud *plays a jig,* "*Father O'Flynn*". Deirdre *starts to dance.* Perry *dances with her.* Miss Archie *moves the card table up* RC. *Everyone claps their hands in time to the music.* Deirdre *suddenly stops and gives a little cry.* Perry *supports her.* Maud *stops playing.* Lotta *rises*)

(*She clutches her heart. In a faint voice*) Mother of God, it's happening —it's happening to me.

(Perry *and* Miss Archie *lift* Deirdre *on to the sofa.* Estelle *rises, crosses to the sofa, kneels beside Deirdre and supports her head*)

Lotta. Brandy—quickly. (*She goes to the desk and pours some brandy into a glass*)
May. You'd better telephone for Dr Jevons, Perry.

(Perry *runs off* L. Lotta *takes the brandy to the sofa and tries to force a little between Deirdre's lips. After a moment or two she desists and* Estelle *wipes Deirdre's mouth gently with her handkerchief*)

Lotta (*feeling for Deirdre's pulse*) I don't think there's much that Dr Jevons could do.
Cora (*rising*) You don't mean—you don't mean . . . ?
Lotta. I'm not sure, but I think so.

(*Everyone stands in silence for a moment looking at Deirdre.* Estelle *bursts into tears.* May *goes to the sofa, takes Deirdre's hands and folds them on her breast, then straightens herself*)

May. The luck of the Irish.

CURTAIN

SCENE—*The same. A Sunday afternoon in the following June.*
The furniture is back in its normal positions, and beyond the french windows the Solarium can be seen in all its glory.

Before the CURTAIN *rises, the music "Waiting in the Wings" is heard.*

When the CURTAIN *rises, it is a sunny afternoon.* ESTELLE, BONITA *and* CORA *are sitting in the Solarium, enjoying the afternoon sun.* MAY *is seated* LC, *working on her embroidery.* LOTTA *is seated on the sofa, reading. After a moment or two she closes the book firmly and puts it on the coffee-table. The music fades.*

LOTTA. Well, I finished it. What on earth do you suppose induced her to write it?

MAY. She couldn't have written it. Marion Brodie is incapable of writing a postcard.

LOTTA (*picking up her knitting*) Well, whoever did write it is certainly highly imaginative. (*She knits*)

MAY. It's a tissue of lies from beginning to end.

LOTTA. I enjoyed the first chapters about her childhood. She says that one of her earliest memories was the crunch of carriage wheels on the drive when mummy and daddy came home from the opera.

MAY. She was born over a tobacconist's shop in the Wilton Road.

LOTTA. Do you think we should write our memoirs, May?

MAY. I most certainly do not.

LOTTA. At least they'd be more interesting than Marion Brodie's. Think of all that we could remember.

MAY. Think of all that we can't forget.

LOTTA. Now then, May—none of that.

(CORA *rises and comes into the room*)

CORA (*crossing to* R) I can't bear sitting under that ghastly glass another minute. (*She exits* R *into the television room*)

MAY. Cora was always a grumbler, even when she was doing quite well. Nothing ever satisfied her.

LOTTA. Do you know, she and I only played together once—that was with Hilary at the *Adelphi* in the twenties. She wore several ropes of pearls and an astrakhan hat.

MAY. She always had delusions of grandeur.

LOTTA. I suspect that she hates being here more than any of us.

MAY (*with a note of bitterness*) I wouldn't be too sure of that?

LOTTA (*curiously*) Do you still hate it—so very much?

MAY (*putting down her embroidery*) Still hate it? Yes, Lotta, I do. I hate it with all my heart and soul. I have tried to be resigned, and even pretended to myself that I was succeeding, but it wasn't

true, it's never been true for a moment. I am formally grateful for
being housed and fed, but I resent every minute of every day,
and every meal that is provided for me chokes me with humilia-
tion. I was always over-proud, which was one of the reasons that
I was never very popular in the theatre, but worse, far worse than
my pride, was my stupid improvidence. For that I am paying a
bitter price and the bitterest part of it is that I know I have only
myself to blame for my contemptible destiny. (*She takes up her
work*) And now, if you don't mind, I should like to change the
subject.

LOTTA (*with a smile*) I see you haven't entirely lost your
arrogance, May. You still like to dictate terms.

MAY. What do you mean?

LOTTA. I might not want to change the subject. I, too, might
wish to bare my soul a little and discuss the carelessness and the
follies and the idiocies that have brought me low.

MAY (*searchingly*) Do you?

LOTTA. No, dear, I don't. I am resigned, you see, and fairly
content.

MAY. I suppose it's a question of temperament.

LOTTA. Are you implying that you possess more of that dubious
asset than I do?

MAY. I'm not implying anything.

LOTTA (*thoughtfully*) Perhaps it is because I always played
gentler parts than you. I was always a dreadfully sweet actress.
I made my first success as Cordelia. I was a very good Cordelia.

MAY. One of the most pompous and disagreeable girls Shakespeare ever wrote.

LOTTA (*laughing*) All right, May—you win.

(*The front-door bell rings*)

MAY. I wonder who that can be.

LOTTA. Probably Osgood.

(DOREEN *enters from the kitchen and exits* R *in the hall*)

MAY. He generally comes straight in. The front door's not
locked.

LOTTA. Perhaps it's some of the committee.

MAY. I hope to heaven it isn't. They're always so over-
poweringly cheerful.

(DOREEN *enters and crosses to* C)

DOREEN. It's a gentleman to see you, Miss Bainbridge.

LOTTA (*surprised*) To see me?

DOREEN. Yes. He said it was important.

LOTTA. Did he give any name?

DOREEN. Yes. Mr Alan Bennet.

(LOTTA *puts her hand to her throat for a moment and closes her eyes*)

Lotta. Oh! (*With an effort*) Ask him to come in, Doreen.
Doreen. Okay, miss.

(Doreen *exits* R *in the hall*)

May (*rising; concerned*) Lotta—it isn't—it can't be . . . ?
Lotta (*rising*) I'm afraid it is.
May (*putting her work in its bag*) I'd better leave you. (*She hangs the bag on the arm of her chair*)
Lotta (*moving to the piano and putting her knitting on it*) No, no—please don't—not for a moment.

(Doreen *enters* R *in the hall and stands to one side*.

ALAN BENNET *enters* R *in the hall and comes into the room. He is in his late forties. He is neatly dressed but there is an indefinable quality of failure about him. His manner is nervous. He looks at* May, *first, then recognizes* Lotta)

Alan. Hullo, Mother.

(Doreen *exits to the kitchen*)

Lotta. Alan—what an extraordinary surprise—I mean—I had no idea you were in England.
Alan. I flew in from Toronto yesterday. (*He goes to Lotta and kisses her*)
Lotta. May—this is my son—Miss May Davenport.
May (*moving* c) How do you do?
Alan (*moving to* R *of May and nervously shaking her hand*) I've certainly heard your name before, Miss Davenport.

(Lotta *crosses to* LC)

May. How very kind of you to say so. I'll leave you now, Lotta.
Lotta. No, please don't. Alan and I can easily talk in the garden or somewhere.
May (*crossing to* R) Nonsense! I'll join Cora in the television room. I don't really care for television but I'm persevering. Good-bye for the moment, Mr Bennet.
Alan. I hope we meet again.
May. Perhaps you will be staying to tea, in which case we are bound to.

(May *exits* R *to the television room*)

Lotta (*after a slight pause*) Sit down, Alan.

(Alan *sits on the sofa at the upstage end*)

Have a cigarette?
Alan. I'm afraid I don't smoke.
Lotta. How wise. I never stop .(*She takes a cigarette from the box on the coffee-table, lights it, then sits in the armchair* LC)

ALAN. Well—well—well!

LOTTA (*with a faint smile*) Well—well—well—indeed!

ALAN. You look splendid, Mother, you really do—I'd have known you anywhere.

LOTTA. I doubt that—thirty-three years is a long time.

ALAN (*guiltily*) Yes—yes, it is—isn't it?

LOTTA (*with an effort*) How is your wife?

ALAN. Cynthia? She's fine.

LOTTA. I'm so glad.

ALAN. She's put on a bit of weight, you know, but I suppose that's only to be expected.

LOTTA. Yes—I suppose it is.

ALAN. She sent you her love.

LOTTA. Thank you—thank you very much.

ALAN. She was quite envious of me coming back home; she's never been out of Canada in her life, you know.

LOTTA. No—I didn't know.

ALAN. She was born in Winnipeg and then her whole family moved to Montreal in nineteen twenty-eight.

LOTTA. Is it large?

ALAN. Winnipeg?

LOTTA. No—her family.

ALAN. Yes—she has three sisters, and a brother in Ecuador.

LOTTA. I'm never quite sure where Ecuador is.

ALAN. It's in South America, between Colombia and Peru.

LOTTA. Oh. (*She pauses*) Have you any children?

ALAN (*rising*) Oh, yes, indeed—three. (*He takes out his wallet and extracts some snapshots*) I've brought some snapshots to show you. (*He kneels beside Lotta*) I'm afraid they're not very good but they'll give you an idea.

LOTTA. I'll put on my glasses. (*She puts her glasses on*)

ALAN (*handing her a snapshot*) That's Joan—she's the baby. When that was taken she was only three.

LOTTA. She looks a sweet little thing.

ALAN (*showing her another snapshot*) That's Eileen, she's at boarding-school.

LOTTA (*scrutinizing it*) A nice sensible face. Does she have to wear those glasses?

ALAN. Yes. She had an astigmatism. They're supposed to correct it.

LOTTA. Poor child, let's hope they do.

ALAN (*producing a third snapshot*) And this is Ronnie, the eldest. He's quite grown up. He's going to be a chartered accountant.

LOTTA. How tall he is, isn't he?

ALAN. Nearly six foot already. He has a wonderful head for figures.

LOTTA. He's fortunate. (*She returns the snapshots to Alan, and turns away, finding the whole situation too much of a strain*)

(ALAN *rises and crosses to the sofa*)

Why didn't you let me know you were coming?

ALAN. I wanted it to be a surprise.

LOTTA (*dryly*) You got your wish. It is.

ALAN. A not too unpleasant one, I hope?

LOTTA (*with a sigh*) Oh, Alan—why on earth *did* you come?

ALAN. I came—to get you out of this place. (*He sits on the sofa at the upstage end*) I had no idea you were in it until a friend of Cynthia's sent her a cutting from the *Sunday Clarion*. It was months old, of course, but that was the first we knew of it. Cynthia was terribly upset, really she was.

LOTTA. Why?

ALAN. Well, hang it—you are her mother-in-law, after all.

LOTTA. We've never set eyes on each other in our lives.

ALAN. That's not her fault.

LOTTA. I didn't say it was. I was merely stating a fact. I only heard from her once and that was seventeen years ago, just after you were married.

ALAN. Well, at any rate, we had a long talk over the whole situation.

LOTTA. Situation?

ALAN. Well, you living here, in a charity home. I had no idea, neither of us had, that things had gone so badly wrong with you.

LOTTA. Things haven't gone so badly wrong with me as all that. I'm quite content here. It's a very comfortable house.

ALAN. Why didn't you write to me when—when the break-up happened?

LOTTA. I think I'd mislaid your address.

ALAN. You're being very hard, Mother. I'm trying to do my best. Please help me.

LOTTA. It was kind of you to come, Alan. At least, I think it was—I'm not even sure of that.

ALAN. I am your son.

LOTTA. Yes, I know. Does that sound as strange to you as it does to me?

ALAN. I'm sorry for having hurt you all those years ago, please believe me.

LOTTA. I believe you, Alan. I'm sorry, too. I expect there were faults on both sides, but I think it is a little late now to try to bridge the gulf. I'm a selfish old woman and set in my ways.

(ALAN *rises and takes a letter from his pocket*)

ALAN. Here's a letter from Cynthia. (*He hands the letter to Lotta*) She asked me to give it to you.

LOTTA. Thank you. (*She opens the letter and reads it*)

ALAN (*moving to the french windows*) She means every word of it. (*He moves to the fireplace, turns and watches Lotta*)

(LOTTA *finishes reading the letter and puts it carefully back into the envelope*)

LOTTA. It's a very kind letter. I'll write to her tomorrow.

ALAN. Do you agree with what she says?

LOTTA (*looking at him*) Do you?

ALAN. Of course. That's why I'm here.

(LOTTA *rises distractedly and goes up* R)

LOTTA. This is a dreadfully difficult moment, Alan—full of sadness and regret and a sort of hopelessness. (*She moves down* R) I can't find any words to deal with it. I wish you hadn't come— I wish you'd stayed out there in your own life and left me to finish mine here in my own way, in peace and quiet.

ALAN (*moving down* LC) Living out your last years on public charity.

LOTTA (*moving down* RC) Does that sound so very humiliating to you?

ALAN (*irritably*) Of course it does. Cynthia was genuinely horrified when she heard it, so was Myrtle.

LOTTA. Myrtle?

ALAN. Cynthia's sister. She's married to one of the most prominent gynaecologists in Toronto.

LOTTA. How convenient.

ALAN (*turning away in exasperation*) Please try to see my point, Mother.

LOTTA. I see it clearly enough, dear. (*She moves up* RC) Cynthia suggests in her letter that I come and live with you both. That would be private charity. Is there so much difference between that and the public sort?

ALAN. Of course there is. You are my mother. There is no question of charity.

LOTTA (*with a slight smile*) You keep on making almost defiant statements. "I am your son." "You are my mother." Do you really believe that they mean much?

ALAN. I'm doing my best to prove to you that I believe it.

LOTTA. Yes—yes—I know you are, and I am being very churlish and disagreeable. (*She sits on the sofa*) But it won't work, my dear, really it won't. You and I may be mother and son in actual fact, but spiritually we're two strangers shouting to each other across a void of thirty-three years. When you were young we managed to draw close to each other every now and then, but not for long—your father saw to that.

ALAN (*challengingly*) It wasn't all father's fault.

LOTTA. I never said it was. It was mine, too, and also the fault of circumstances. I was away on tour a great deal and beginning to do well in the theatre. Your father, on the other hand, wasn't. He was a very jealous man, not only personally jealous but professionally jealous.

(ALAN *makes a movement of protest*)

I don't blame him for taking you from me. Knowing his character, it was inevitable. But I couldn't have stopped working then even if I had wanted to. If I had we should all three have starved.

ALAN. There's not much point in raking all that up again, is there?

LOTTA. I think it is important that we should both remember exactly where we stood in a very critical moment of our lives. After the divorce you had to make your choice and you made it. You were certainly old enough to know your own mind.

(ALAN *starts to speak*)

Please don't think that I'm reproaching you, I'm not. I'm merely trying to make you see that certain gestures in life are irrevocable.

ALAN. Do you mean that you won't come, that you won't accept the home that Cynthia and I offer you?

LOTTA (*wearily*) Of course I won't, my dear. It would be insupportable for everyone concerned. You must know that in your heart—you must. One day, if I live long enough and you can afford it, I would like to come to you for a visit and meet Cynthia and—and my grandchildren.

(ALAN *crosses to the sofa and sits on it, downstage of Lotta. He cannot completely conceal his relief*)

ALAN. Mother—please don't be hasty over this. Think it over carefully before you decide absolutely.

LOTTA. Very well.

ALAN. I shall be here until the end of next week. I have some business to do for my firm.

LOTTA. I don't even know what your firm is.

ALAN. It's called the "O.T.B." The Ontario Travel Bureau. It's a steady income, nothing spectacular, but there are chances of advancement—and if I hang on long enough I get a pension when I retire.

LOTTA. Like me.

ALAN (*rising and moving* C) I think I'd better be going now. I've got a taxi outside.

LOTTA (*rising and moving to Alan*) Wouldn't you like to send it away and stay to tea? We're quite a cheerful little group.

ALAN (*embarrassed*) No, really—I'd rather not. (*He hesitates*) Shall I come and see you again?

LOTTA (*looking at him; her eyes suddenly filling with tears*) Yes, dear, do, please do, just once more.

ALAN. Mother . . .

LOTTA (*warding him off*) Go now—go at once—there's a dear boy.

ALAN. But, Mother . . .

LOTTA. Please do as I ask. It's been rather a shock seeing you again so—so—unexpectedly. (*She gains control of herself*) Where can I get in touch with you?

ALAN. I'm at the *Cumberland Hotel*.

LOTTA. The *Cumberland*. I'll remember. Good-bye, dear. (*She kisses him, holds him tightly for a moment, then pushes him gently away*) Go now.

ALAN. Will Wednesday or Thursday be all right?

LOTTA. Wednesday or Thursday will be fine.

ALAN. Let's say Thursday, then. If I came about noon I could take you out to lunch.

LOTTA. Yes. That would be lovely. I shall look forward to it.

(ALAN *moves towards the hall*)

Au revoir.

ALAN. *Au revoir*, then.

(ALAN *smiles a little nervously at Lotta, then exits in the hall to* R. LOTTA *sinks on to the sofa, buries her face in her hands and bursts into tears.*

MAY *enters from the television room. She sees Lotta crying, hesitates for a moment, then goes to her*)

MAY. Lotta, don't cry—please don't cry.

LOTTA (*in a muffled voice*) I'll be all right in a minute.

MAY. Why did he come here?

LOTTA. He brought me a letter from his wife inviting me to go and live with them in Canada. It was quite a kind letter—and very carefully written.

MAY. And you said "No"?

LOTTA (*sitting up; without emotion*) Yes. I said "no".

MAY. I see.

(*There is a slight pause*)

(*She puts a hand on Lotta's shoulder*) Is there anything I can do to help?

LOTTA (*resting her hand for a moment on May's hand*) Yes, dear May. You can hand me my knitting—it's on the piano.

(*The sound of a motor-cycle horn is heard.* MAY *moves to the piano and picks up Lotta's knitting*)

MAY. That's Perry. He'll be able to tell us how rehearsals are going for the matinée. (*She gives the knitting to Lotta*)

(MAUD *and* ALMINA *appear in the Solarium*)

LOTTA. Thank you. If anyone had told me a year ago that a time would come when I should really enjoy knitting, I should have thought they were mad.

MAY. It's a very pretty colour. What's it going to be?

LOTTA. A bed-jacket. The one I have is Alice-blue and too *ingénue*. It's also falling to pieces.

(ESTELLE *and* BONITA *rise and come into the room.* ALMINA *and* MAUD *follow them in.* ALMINA *goes to the easy chair down* L *and sits.* MAUD *moves to the piano.* BONITA *crosses to the card table.* ESTELLE *goes to the fire-stool and sits.* MAY *sits in the armchair* LC)

ALMINA. It's really almost too hot there. You'd hardly believe it, would you?

(CORA *enters from the television room*)

CORA. That damned television has started wobbling again. Fortunately, it's only a Welsh choir.
MAUD (*complacently*) Miss Archie will fix it.
BONITA. Time for a game of backgammon before tea, Cora?

(PERRY *enters* R *in the hall. He carries a small parcel*)

PERRY. *Bonjour, Mesdames—comment ça va?*
BONITA. Ever so *très bien*, thanks.

(CORA *and* BONITA *open the card table.* PERRY *crosses to May and gives her a small parcel*)

PERRY. Many happy returns. (*He kisses May*)
MAY (*severely*) Perry! You are breaking the rules again. You know perfectly well that any mention of birthdays is forbidden in this house.
PERRY. It's just a little something to make you smell pretty.

(MAUD *crosses to* R *of* BONITA. LOTTA *puts Alan's letter in her knitting bag, and knits*)

BONITA. Many happy returns, May. Why didn't you tell us?

(*The others murmur* "Many happy returns, happy birthday", *etc.*)

MAY. Thank you—thank you all very much. (*She opens the parcel and holds up a very small bottle of* "Arpège" *perfume*) Oh, Perry, you really shouldn't have. I am most displeased—and very touched. (*She kisses him*)

(PERRY *pats May's hand affectionately, then turns to the others*)

PERRY. Has Topsy Baskerville arrived yet?
BONITA. No. Miss Archie went up this morning. She's bringing her down on the two-five, so they ought to be here any minute.
MAUD. Poor old Topsy. I wonder how she feels.

(CORA *goes to the desk and collects a backgammon board*)

CORA. There's no need to wonder. We all know how she feels.
BONITA. I was with her at the *Hippodrome* during the first war, in nineteen fifteen. She sang "Oh, Mr Kaiser".

MAUD. Oh, yes—I remember that. (*She marches down* R *and sings*)

"OH, MR KAISER"

Oh, Mr Kaiser,
See your legal adviser,
You've bitten off much more than you can chew.

(*She marches to the piano, sits and plays*)

For when Mr Tommy Atkins comes a-marching to Berlin,
You'll be gibbering like a monkey in the Zoo.
Have a banana!

(BONITA *joins in the singing*)

BONITA⎱
MAUD ⎰ (*together*)

Oh, Mr Kaiser,
When you're older and wiser
You'll learn some things you never learnt at school.
When we've wound up the watch on your dear old Rhine,
You're going to look a Potsdam fool.

(ESTELLE *crosses to the tub chair and sits*)

MAY. Who is this Topsy? I've never heard of her.
PERRY. Topsy Baskerville. She was in musical comedy and revue mostly.
MAY. Poor thing. So exhausting.

(CORA *lays out the backgammon board on the card table*)

PERRY. She's a sweet old girl. You'll love her.
LOTTA. I'm sure we shall, Perry dear. I'm sure we shall. (*She rises*) I expect that's exactly what you said a year ago when I arrived.
BONITA. Yes, I expect we did. Fancy, a whole year ago. It doesn't seem possible, does it?
LOTTA (*crossing to* MAY) I remember I was in deep despair——

(MAY *holds Lotta's hand*)

—lonely and hopeless and feeling as though I were going to prison. (*She crosses to the fireplace*) And now, after a year in prison, I feel suddenly free. Isn't that curious?

(*The front door slams. The remaining lines are spoken almost simultaneously through the song*)

MISS ARCHIE (*off*) Come along, this way, Miss Baskerville.

(CORA *moves to the foot of the stairs.*
MISS ARCHIE *enters from the hall and stands* R. MAUD *starts to play softly and sing* "Oh, Mr Kaiser"

TOPSY BASKERVILLE *enters from the hall, looks around timidly, then recognizes her song)*

TOPSY (*after a pause*) Why, that's my song. (*She moves slowly* RC)
BONITA. Hullo, Topsy—it's me—Bonita.

TOPSY *turns, recognizes Bonita, runs to her and embraces her. While* MAUD *and* BONITA *continue to sing* "*Oh, Mr Kaiser*", TOPSY *greets Estelle and then Perry.* PERRY *introduces Topsy to May and Lotta as—*

the CURTAIN *falls*

FURNITURE AND PROPERTY LIST

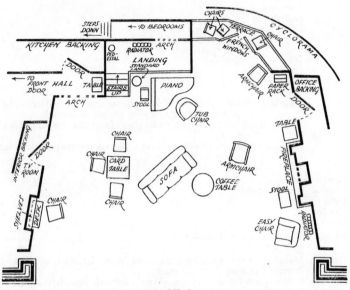

ACT I

SCENE I

On stage—Desk. *On it:* patience cards, 2 packs playing cards, ink, pens, box
with cigarettes, matches, ashtray, notepaper, envelopes,
blotter, book

On shelves: books, including paper-backs

Desk chair

On wall down R: electric wall-bracket

Waste-paper basket

Table (RC). *On it:* 2 packs cards, hands set; 2 scoring cards, 2 pencils,
ashtray

3 upright chairs

Piano. *On it:* book, matches, 2 Sunday newspapers, ashtray, music

Piano stool

Standard lamp

Tub chair

Sofa. *On it:* cushions, copy of *The Times*

Coffee-table. *On it:* copies of the *Sunday Times*, the *Sunday Express*,
the *News of the World*, the *Sunday Dispatch*; book for
Bonita, box with cigarettes, matches, ashtray

Armchair (LC). *On it:* embroidery bag with canvas, needles, wools,
scissors, thimble, spectacles

Armchair (*up* L). *On it:* 2 Sunday newspapers

Paper-rack. *In it:* paper and magazines

Occasional table

85

On mantelpiece: clock, ornaments, vases of roses, matches, ashtray
Coal scuttle with coal
Fire grate
Fender
Fire-irons
Footstool
Fire-stool
Hearth rug
Easy chair (*down* L). *On it:* cushions
Over mantelpiece: oil painting of Ellen Terry
                  2 electric wall-brackets
Window curtains
Carpet on floor
Radiator (*down* L)
Stair carpet
On landing: carpet, pedestal with bust, radiator, framed playbills,
              picture, fire extinguisher, electric wall-brackets
In hall: dumb-waiter, carpet, small glass chandelier. *On wall:* clock,
           picture
On terrace: 3 garden chairs. *On them:* 3 Sunday newspapers, knitting
              in bag, comic paper
Light switches up C, on landing, below door up L

French windows open
Window curtains open
Light fittings off
Fire on
Doors closed

Off stage—Bunch of violets (OSGOOD)
           Suitcase (DORA)

Personal—MAUD: horn-rimmed glasses, large bag. *In it:* cigarettes, matches
         BONITA: handbag. *In it:* compact
         PERRY: crash helmet, goggles, gloves, case with cigarettes, lighter
         LOTTA: handbag, gloves
         DORA: handbag

                          SCENE 2

Strike—Everything from coffee-table
         Everything from card table
         Newspapers
         Flowers
         Helmet, goggles and gloves
Fold card table and set close behind sofa
Set chairs RC close into card table
Replace fire-stool at fireplace
Close desk
Close piano
Tidy room generally
Set—fresh flowers

French windows closed
Window curtains closed
Fire on
Doors closed
Hall light on
Landing brackets on
Standard lamp on

Off stage—Tray. *On it:* 2 plates sandwiches (DOREEN)
    Glass of water (DOREEN)
    Tray. *On it:* 8 bowls of soup (DOREEN)
Personal—MISS ARCHIE: watch

ACT II

SCENE 1

Strike—Trays
  Plates
  Soup bowls
  Glass of water
  Flowers
Reset furniture as Act I, Scene 1
Piano open
Card table open
Desk closed
Set—Fresh flowers
  On card table: matches, patience cards
  On coffee-table: book matches, box with cigarettes, ashtray
  In desk: box with cigarettes, ashtray, matches
  On piano: matches
  On mantelpiece: matches
French windows closed
Window curtains open
Fire on
Doors closed
Light fittings off
Off stage—Camera (ZELDA)
    Workbag with embroidery and glasses (MAY)
    Tray with tea things (DOREEN)
Personal—PERRY: lighter
    ZELDA: handbag. *In it:* cigarettes, notebook, pencil

SCENE 2

Strike—Everything from card table
Set—On armchair LC: May's bag with spectacles
French windows closed
Window curtains closed
Fire on
Doors closed
Fittings off
Off stage—Packet of cigarettes, lighter (MAUD)
    Blanket (SARITA)
    Tray. *On it:* 9 glasses, jug of water (LOTTA)
    ½ bottle whisky (BONITA)
Personal—ESTELLE: matches

SCENE 3

Strike—Tray, bottle of whisky, glasses
  Flowers
Set—On coffee-table: ashtray, box with cigarettes, matches
  On desk: patience cards, box with cigarettes, matches

> *On sofa: Sunday Clarion* for Bonita
> *Sunday Times* for Deirdre
> *On easy chair down* L: *Sunday Clarion* for Lotta
> *On armchair* LC: May's work-bag
> *On armchair up* L: work-bag and knitting for Estelle
> *On tub chair:* newspaper for Almina
> Fresh flowers

Fold card table against back of sofa
Open desk
Replace fire extinguisher
French windows closed
Window curtains open
Fire on
Doors closed
Fittings off

Off stage—Bunch of violets (OSGOOD)
Suitcase (MISS ARCHIE)

ACT III

SCENE I

Strike—Flowers
Newspapers
3 upright chairs
Everything from coffee-table
Everything from card table
Work-bags

Move card table to RC
Move sofa to R
Move coffee-table to LC

Set—*On sofa:* wrapping papers
On coffee-table: wrapping papers
On card table: empty cracker box, wrapping papers
Christmas tree and lights up L
On floor up L: wrapping papers
On desk: tray with brandy, other bottles, glasses
On mantelpiece: Christmas cards
On piano: Christmas cards, wrapping paper
On pictures: holly
Behind clock: holly
Over mantelpiece: paper decorations
In hall: paper decorations
On landing: paper decorations
Fresh flowers

French windows closed
Window curtains closed
Doors closed
Fire on
Christmas tree lights on
Wall-bracket R off
Wall-brackets L off
Hall light on
Landing bracket on
Standard lamp on

Off stage—Champagne crate (ZELDA)
        Tray. *On it:* 12 cups of coffee, 12 saucers, 12 coffee spoons, sugar
               basin (DOREEN)
        Paper caps (LADIES)
        Tray. *On it:* 12 tumblers (MISS ARCHIE)
        2 opened bottles of champagne (PERRY)
        Opened bottle of champagne (MISS ARCHIE)
Personal—ZELDA: envelope. *In it:* cheque
        ESTELLE: handkerchief

SCENE 2

Strike—Christmas tree
      Cards
      Decorations and holly
      Trays, bottles and glasses
      Flowers
Reset furniture as Act I, Scene 2
Set—Solarium
      On sofa: book and knitting for Lotta
      On desk: backgammon board
      On coffee-table: box with cigarettes, ashtray, matches, Lotta's knitting bag
      Fresh flowers
French windows open
Window curtains open
Doors closed
Fires on
Light fittings off
Off stage—Parcel. *In it:* bottle of "Arpège" (PERRY)
Personal—ALAN: letter, wallet. *In it:* snapshots
        LOTTA: glasses

Any character costumes or wigs needed in the
performance of this play can be hired from
CHARLES H. FOX LTD, 25 SHELTON STREET,
LONDON WC2H 9HX

LIGHTING PLOT

Property Fittings Required—fire, standard lamp, 4 electric candle wall-brackets, small glass chandelier, Christmas tree lights

Interior. A lounge. The same scene throughout

THE APPARENT SOURCES OF LIGHT ARE—in daytime, french windows up L; at night: 2 wall-brackets L, 1 wall-bracket on landing up C, 1 wall-bracket down R, a standard lamp up C; a small glass chandelier in hall up R

THE MAIN ACTING AREAS ARE: the whole stage

ACT I SCENE 1 A June afternoon
To open: General effect of summer sunshine
           Fittings off
           Fire on

No cues

ACT I SCENE 2 Night
To open: Dark outside windows
           On-stage lighting checked
           Hall light on
           Standard lamp on
           Landing bracket on
           Fire on

Cue 1 DOREEN switches on bracket R   (page 22)
       Snap in bracket R
       Snap in covering lights

Cue 2 MISS ARCHIE switches on brackets L   (page 22)
       Snap in brackets L
       Snap in covering lights

ACT II SCENE 1 A September afternoon
To open: General effect of sunshine
           Fittings off
           Fire on

No cues

ACT II SCENE 2 Night
To open: The stage in darkness
           Fittings off
           Fire on

Cue 3 BONITA: "Miss Archie!"   (page 45)
       Switch on strip outside door L

Cue 4 MAY switches on landing bracket   (page 45)
       Snap in landing bracket
       Snap in covering lights

Cue 5 CORA switches on brackets L   (page 45)
       Snap in brackets L
       Snap in covering lights

Cue 6 BONITA *switches on bracket* R   (page 46)
       Snap in bracket R
       Snap in covering lights

Cue* 7   CORA switches off bracket R   (page 51)
Snap out bracket R
Snap out covering lights

Cue 8   CORA *switches off landing bracket*   (page 51)
Snap out landing bracket
Snap out covering lights

ACT II   SCENE 3   Afternoon
To open: Effect of dull daylight
Fire on
Fittings off

No cues

ACT III   SCENE 1   Night
To open: Dark outside windows
On-stage lighting checked
Hall light on
Standard lamp on
Landing bracket on
Christmas tree lights on
Fire lit

Cue 9   DOREEN switches on bracket R   (page 62)
Snap in bracket R
Snap in covering lights

Cue 10   MISS ARCHIE switches on brackets L   (page 62)
Snap in brackets L
Snap in covering lights

ACT III   SCENE 2   A June afternoon
To open: General effect of summer sunshine
Fittings off
Fire on

No cues

EFFECTS PLOT

ACT I

SCENE 1

Cue 1   Before rise of CURTAIN   (page 2)
          Music of "Waiting in the Wings"

Cue 2   At rise of CURTAIN   (page 2)
          Fade music

Cue 3   CORA: ". . . stopped the show"   (page 7)
          Sound of motor-cycle horn

Cue 4   CORA: "We all loathed it."   (page 10)
          Front-door bell rings

Cue 5   CORA: ". . . no time sense . . ."   (page 10)
          Front door slams

Cue 6   BONITA: ". . . into my shroud."   (page 13)
          Front-door bell rings

SCENE 2

Cue 7   Before rise of CURTAIN   (page 22)
          Music of "Waiting in the Wings"

Cue 8   At rise of CURTAIN   (page 22)
          Fade music

Cue 9   SARITA: ". . . as a hunter."   (page 24)
          Sound of motor horn

ACT II

SCENE 1

Cue 10   Before rise of CURTAIN   (page 30)
          Music of "Waiting in the Wings"

Cue 11   At rise of CURTAIN   (page 30)
          Fade music

Cue 12   Follows above cue   (page 30)
          Front-door bell rings

Cue 13   DOREEN exits R   (page 30)
          Front door slams

Cue 14   ZELDA exits   (page 43)
          Front door slams

SCENE 2

Cue 15   Before rise of CURTAIN   (page 44)
          Music of "Miss Mouse"

Cue 16   At rise of CURTAIN   (page 44)
          Fade music

92